ÅF192122

JULIET SMITH

My Journey of Life

novum 📖 pro

This book is also available as e-book.

www.novum-publishing.co.uk

© 2023 novum publishing

ISBN 978-3-99131-526-1
Editing: Roderick Pritchard-Smith
Cover photo:
Jacob_09 BK | Dreamstime.com
Cover design, layout & typesetting: novum publishing

www.novum-publishing.co.uk

Climate neutral
Print product
ClimatePartner.com/16547-2201-1002

Contents

Chapter 1

Introduction

My name is Juliet Smith. I am currently living in Wimbledon London. I am at the best point in my life to share my story with you about my life span and what has transpired within it for over the past 59 years of my existence on planet earth.

I was born at Hammersmith Hospital London on the 18t of July 1960 to my parents Darcy and Lois Smith who came to London to study with a scholarship from the British Council in Sierra Leone. I have 2 brothers and 2 sisters – namely Daphne, Audrey, Victor and Francis. Francis was an outside child in the family as he was born to another woman with whom my dad was having an affair.

I am torn between two walls in my life as I lived in London until I was 3 years old after which time my parents took me with them back to Sierra Leone where they came from as my dad had to resume official duties after his studies.

In order for my parents to take up their role as a student and working to meet living costs, I was placed with foster parents – Mr and Mrs Rees where I stayed during the week and on Friday evenings my dad would pick me up to spend the weekend with him and mum. I was adjusting very well to this new way of life and getting more acquainted with my foster family, Susan and David.

This early stage of my life I would describe as good as I was exposed to the British culture. When I returned to Sierra Leone with my parents there was a lot of poverty. Food, shelter and clothing was hard to get as my mum who was a teacher in Sierra

Leone was not paid a salary for several months and that caused a strain on our family finances.

I would remember the landlord coming and having to ask for the rent as we seemed to always be in arrears of paying. Food too was scarce, and we had little to feed ourselves with. I lived at home with my sister Audrey and brother Victor together with my mum and dad. Daphne the oldest stayed with my grandmother when my parents travelled to London in 1958 and had lived with her ever since. She did not return to mum and dad on their arrival back in Freetown and she continued living there until grandmother passed away in 2001.

I am an outgoing person, always taking the initiative and acting in a caring and positive manner, as I learnt from an early age to try to adapt to the changes that swept me very rapidly off my feet. Things were harder than anticipated – lack attached itself to me. I would go without the basic needs. I was struggling for survival for the things which everybody takes for granted. My dad was a very busy man and spent much of his time outside the house but unfortunately was not providing for us as a family which is a shame. I was always comparing myself with others, observing that I was very poor having very little or nothing as I was unable to get just the basic things that I needed in life.

This however, on my part, caused me to withdraw a lot. I felt shy and upset at times as my basic needs were not provided for me by my parents. This went on for almost all my life and I seemed to be very disturbed in my mind and spirit as I couldn't cope with the problems life gave me.

Deep down in my heart I was hoping for a better life. Trusting that things would change for the better I lived in this condition until I was 28 years old. During the ages of 3 until 28 I was hoping that a miracle would come my way so that I would be able to return to London to gain a more prosperous life. When we returned to Freetown my foster parents sent a ticket for me to return to London, but my mum declined the offer even though she knew she was unable to care and provide for my basic needs and give me the love and support that was needed.

I attended the Tower Hill Municipal School, Freetown from classes 1 to class 7 and took the selective entrance examination for the Methodist Girls High School and passed. I was admitted to school in 1971. I would say I was an above average scholar at school wanting to learn and increase my knowledge of the outside world. Life is cruel. I used to cry my eyes out a lot in the night thinking that I would struggle to obtain a proper education, but my initiative was so good that I hardly ever lacked purpose in my life. I had lots of friends at school but was subjected to bullying by the much stronger boys.

My parents were strict, and I found it difficult to discuss any problems in my life for fear that it would have an adverse effect on my welfare.

I could not relate to my mother and had to seek advice from others in my surroundings. Even at age 13, when my menstruation started, I had to manage the feelings alone with no one to approach to assist me into how I should be managing myself monthly when these sensations began. My mum was very distant in my life. Not someone I could discuss issues with. She made sure she was always at arm's length when it came to dealing with my problems or anything that might disturb me. I felt lonely and I always felt discriminated against as my brother Victor took all the attention from her. She loved my brother Victor more than all the girls. Audrey and myself were always supportive of him – whenever Victor did something wrong mum never disciplined him but as soon as I did anything wrong, she would get upset and physically beat me with a stick. This was the idea of family life I grew up in – I loved my brother Victor but the role my mother played between us was unacceptable as she sided with Victor if there was a problem between us.

When I was naughty my mum would keep me into a dark room. I hate the dark.

Chapter 2

Family Situation

There was always rivalry and jealousy between my siblings especially my sister Audrey and me. She thought I was doing better than her in life and stabbed me in the back and said all sorts of unkind things about me to others. I was made to be aware of her actions and take precautionary measures. It was not an easy road considering that I was older than her, but I had to be made aware of her bad mouthing to others about me and my relationships with others.

Audrey is the sister I am always careful of as she out of jealousy and malice seems to think that I am doing well in life. Only God keeps me going and providing for my needs. I have no one to relate to other than my heavenly father, when I am in need I pray and ask the good Lord to supply all my needs and God has been supplying my needs through his people. So, although I am faced with bad traits like these from people, I tend to try to caution myself and move away from the situation because there is more to life than just that.

Growing up has not been easy for me with lots of challenges that I face as I live. Audrey steals my relationships and makes sure she has sex with them. There was a guy called Cecil Dull I was dating in my school for a while. Audrey then later took over the relationship, one thing led to another and all I know is that she was planning to get married to him but what happened only God knows. It never materialised and Audrey is my sister – things have changed on the long-rugged road that we have travelled in our quest for satisfaction, but I learned at an early age to forgive and let God fight my battles for me. It is not easy considering that it is my own flesh and blood who is doing this evil to me but as the Lord's prayer says 'forgive us our trespasses as we forgive those that trespass against us'.

I have learnt to let God have his own way in my life and have learned to put the past back in my mind and not bear a grudge or feelings of resentment towards others who offend me. I have learned that in life people may tread on my big toe, but I should be quick and willing to forgive and ask God to have pity upon us all. I had a long-term partner by the name of Osborne Marke. Audrey had sex with him in her house and tended to be very rude to me when approached about this. Osborne was one of my partners, a very selfish and dominating gentleman. He treated me very badly and was always shouting. I ended the relationship when I had had enough of his behaviour and his insensitivity towards to me. He was always bringing me down, talking down to me and making me feel inferior towards him. He never ever loved me; he was using me for his own personal gain. When I realised what his motives were, I ended the relationship. He still wanted to come back to me, but I refused saying the experience I had with him was unfavourable and no way could I go back again with him.

I always gave my best in love to the person I felt attracted to, but it always turned sour. They just used my kind nature and calmness to take advantage of me. I am caring, kind and calm and can become very much attracted in love to someone who I love This was the case for a gentleman called Samue Stronge, my schooldays boyfriend with whom I ended up having a child by the name of Jenner Stronge.

It is a shame that things didn't end up well between us in our relationship because when Jenner was 3 years old, I came back to live in London. I actually met Samue whilst I was still living in Freetown and we got to know each other well and I was hoping that one day we would get married as he was my ideal partner. I trusted him very much and was badly in love with him but unfortunately he was refused entry to London and had to be sent back to Freetown. Shortly after he went, I got news that he had married another woman – this broke my heart. I was truly hoping that he would wait for the application process to go ahead and try to get another ticket to make the journey to London so that we could live as a family and have some more kids together. Samue's family accepted me and was supportive to me and to Jenner at all times.

Relationships with the opposite sex have been on a roller coaster basis. Nothing concrete, only fairy tale syndrome. While I was living in Sierra Leone, I made lots of friends and got to know lots of people. Victor was fortunate to have a scholarship to Norway, after which he was to come to London to study accountancy so he told me not to worry but to be patient so that when he came to London he would send me a one-way ticket to come back to live in London.

This he did on 7th July 1988. I travelled back to London to live and left Jenner, who was 3 years old at the time, with his dad Samue and hoping that they both would join me later. So, one summer when mum was coming to spend a holiday with us I asked her to kindly bring Jenner with her. She agreed and I sent him a ticket and he came to live with me in London.

Six years ago, I fell in love again. This time to Gersham Compaguire Coker. The man of my dream. We are still going out although he does not live in London, yet he is there for me when I need his wise counsel and advice. We are hoping to get married soon and will be able to live together in the same country. He is passionate about life and is a true Christian, a God-fearing man who is after God's own heart. I love him to bits. He is a friend of the family, we met through his friend Olu Williams who suggested to him that he should consider dating me which he pursued ever since and we have been getting on well.

Chapter 3

Living in Sierra Leone

I lived in Sierra Leone with my parents and siblings from ages 3 to 28 years when I came back to live in London. I went to school in Sierra Leone and joined a church fellowship called Bethel Temple with my mum. I was a member of the youth group which meets on Sundays at 5.30pm to 7.00pm in the church called Christ Ambassador. I was very much involved in this groups although I did not actually accept the Lord Jesus Christ as my Lord and saviour until I was 16 years old.

It all happened one day in church during the evening service which starts at 7.00pm. A film was shown called 'Thief in the night'. I was moved to tears and fear swept through me like nobody's business. I was thinking to myself, 'If Christ should come this very moment, I will not make it to heaven even though I have been very faithful in my church attendance but I have never invited Jesus into my heart as my Lord and saviour.' After the film, Pastor Jones called an altar call for those who would like to accept Christ to go forward to the altar. I was so thrilled to move forward with others who had the same connections and surrendered my life to Christ. It was a moving experience for me at the time. I felt so much joy and peace in my heart and thought to myself, 'Well I am saved and will be happy to go up in the sky to meet the Lord in the air,' if Jesus would have come at that precise moment.

I had lots of friends in my youth group, and we met every Sunday afternoon at 1pm at the Connaught Hospital for hospital ministry. A commitment I always long to be a part of. I believe God has blessed me with healing and whenever I pray for the sick, I always witness a sense of positive vibe flowing through my body and see miracles being performed. The sick have been healed and deliverance flowed into the hearts of God's people.

I would join the group at the hospital for the ministration of the Gospel in the church where we sang religious songs, mainly choruses, and read the Bible. After that a short talk given by one of the members of the group and we then move from bed to bed praying for the sick to be made whole through the power of God.

Shortly after I was converted, I was blessed with the baptism of the Holy Spirit with the evidence of speaking in tongues. A blessing to cherish until this day. Then the next baptism by immersion, I was able to go through that process as well.

So being filled with the Holy Spirit equipped me for the proclamation of the Gospel and I was also able to see lots of signs and wonders being performed by my ministry. The sick were healed, the lame walked, the blind saw and a whole lot of miracles took place under the power of intervention from the Holy Spirit.

I have always had a soft spot in my life. Always been very moved to tears and sadness when things do not seem to go as expected but I had faith in the Lord and trusted Him all along the way for his provision and care upon my life and that of my family.

God has been gracious to me, pleasure in mercy doing wonder in my life. I can recall very clearly the fact that I witnessed a miracle in my life while I was preparing my garments for a crusade in 1970 at the stadium. I mistakenly swallowed a needle I was using to mend my clothes that I wanted to wear. I went to the crusade and told the authorities about what had happened. They prayed for me and afterwards I came home. But I was still bearing pain in my throat so I told my mum who took me to hospital but when I was X rayed the film did not show any needle in my body so the doctor prescribed medicines which I was took and said I may have passed it in my faeces as there was no sign of the needle in my body. I give God the glory for his deliverance and healing.

I knew from an early age in my life that God who created me loved me so much that he gave his one and only son to die for my sins. It cannot get any better than that, only faith and belief in the Lord Jesus Christ keeps me going in life, as all things are possible to those who believe. Even though I felt distant from my mum, yet the Father's love surrounded me and is still with me even to this day. Nothing I can do in this life will repay God for his tender mercies and goodness towards me. He adopted me into his family, and I am loved by God who is my creator and the redeemer of my soul.

My mission in life is not complete until I accept his full forgiveness for my sins and that of those who hurt me painfully. God cares for my needs; he satisfies and every need he supplies. He is the reason I live. No other way to heaven except through his son Jesus Christ. I have accepted his love in my heart, and I am truly saved by the power of his spirit which guides and directs my faith. I tend to be withdrawn when I face challenges in my life, but the light of God keeps shining within me and the spirit has always been faithful to me, cheering me on and enabling me to take necessary action in prayer and praise to a God who meets my every need. I try to motivate myself in those challenging situations that I face because problems can be suffered and God wants my attention more than anything else, so when I am faced with difficulty, I pray a lot and fast at certain times according to the lead of God's Holy Spirit in my life and God has been coming through for me through answered prayers. It is not an easy road but with Christ in the vessel I am always smiling at the storm. The flavour of life is raging high, but God is greater than the power of hell. He knows what I can endure, and he has been giving me grace to follow him daily. I like to pray a lot because when I pray God answers. His promises for me are sure and he likes it when I kneel in prayer with my request. God has done it in times past and will certainly do it again for me also and in the future if I keep on trusting in him and always pray to him.

The Bible is my guide and I try to read it ever so often to remind me of God's love to me and his promises are always true. No evil will befall me and I know that God will do what no man can do for me in this life.

I lost my dad in 1993 and since his death I have always held on to God as my heavenly father. It is not easy, but God satisfies every longing in my heart. I was living in London at the time of his death and was unable to travel to Sierra Leone for the funeral. I loved my earth father a lot as he showed me fatherly love. It was sad to part with him in this way, but God knows best and one day we will be united in the heavenly realms of life. He tries to be protective of me. I could remember very well that when my male friends would come to visit me at my house, especially friends from my youth groups, it would be very hard asking them to go away and leave me alone. But I would be very sad. I said they are only my friends from church. Dad loved all his children equally. He never showed favour to one more than the other, we all feel the fatherly love he showed to us. I am very grateful to God for giving me a father who understands me and one I can talk to if I am in trouble of any kind. He is a great and famous man one who has the heart for the things of God and was a strict disciplinarian. He died on Jenner's birthday, 24 January 1993. Jenner was 8 years old at that time. This sadness overwhelms me. I know he is in heaven watching over me.

I was also part of the scripture Yaidon in my secondary school – Methodist girls' high school where we were taught the word of God and how to be a good citizen in our community.

I also represented my school at the head office in Liverpool Street during some vital sessions and on Saturdays and I was involved with Youth for Christ that met every Saturday at the Christ church basement. It was great fun seeing other people who I felt acquainted with at these meetings. We met for fellowship and prayer and a time to study the Bible so that we could become better citizens in our world of duty.

Life was great fun during those days as we got on very well with each other. I made lots of friends during this and some of these people are in contact with me even until this day. Most of us have travelled abroad for a better life and have since kept in touch.

My dad was an organist at Christ church and went to church with Audrey and Victor while I went to church with mum to Bethel Temple, Tower Hill, Freetown Sierra Leone. My dad insisted that I should be confirmed so I did that, and it was a pleasant experience again to publicly declare my faith in the Lord Jesus Christ as my saviour and Lord.

The senior liaison officers would come to school to give us a talk and then after school on certain days of the week we would go to the head office at Liverpool Street for fellowship with other people from other schools. It was great to represent my school at those meetings and I felt proud of myself there. We would sing and make a contribution from our school in songs, pray and read scriptures for the day. It was a blessing to be part of the group and what God was doing in that part of the world.

I did not have money, but I had the spirit of God in my life that is keeping me going in life. Life was good in those days as I didn't worry about anything in life especially things that endangered my wellbeing. I was also involved in street evangelic going door to door sharing the good news of Jesus to the lost and unsaved with my youth group. We would meet in church, pray and then go out in twos to the public. Many people came to know God through our visits in their homes to share the gospel of faith to the lost and dying and many signs followed our ministry with healings for the sick. Jesus moved upon the hearts of people, and we saw many come to faith because of their interaction with the outside world.

God moved behind the scenes in my life, and I am thankful to him for the great opportunity to serve God in this way. He has never failed me and even though financially I was unable to obtain the things I needed for my wellbeing as my parents could just not afford to provide for my needs. I learnt at an early age to learn to trust in God and pray to him every day and commit my ways unto the Lord and he would come through for me through various mediums he chose fit to perform his actions. My life is in his hands, he promises to never leave me nor forsake me, and I trust in hm for my daily bread. Nothing is impossible with God. What he has done for others he will do for me, and I take him at his word that if one asks, we shall receive. So, I am in the business of always putting my request before God and trusting him to make a way for me. He has never failed once yet. He is the reason I live. No other person can do this for me. He is all sufficient, he knows me when I wake up in the morning and when I go to sleep and keeps watch over me all day long. God promise me that he will do a new thing in my life and every day I look forward to him for what he has in store for me for that day. Praying and anticipating that he will provide for my needs daily.

God speaks to me through his word the Bible and through an audience that I recognise and came to realise that he is speaking in accent loud and clear. He stirs my heart to forward and open doors on my behalf. He is the motivator for my existence, and I am very grateful that he has chosen me for such a time as this. He is my saviour, my creator and his spirit lives within my heart guiding me through this life journey. Nothing is impossible with God. He satisfies and has been my helper in ages past.

I have faith in God that no matter what I am facing now he can see me through it all. I have learned to trust in Him alone because when I look to people, they fail but he promises his love and care to me and has never failed me yet. His promises to me are sure and perfect in all his ways. No other people can beat his actions towards me. He is the head of my life. I am standing in the promises of Christ my saviour as he paid it all for my sins at Calvary.

My spiritual life has not been a bed of roses: Since I found God I have followed the devices of my sinful lust and drifted away from the fold in my 20s but God's love was very faithful, he never stopped asking me to come back to God. He assures me still of his love and care at those dark moments of my life. I have been involved in sin of all sorts. The sin of fornication and had a child out of wedlock as a result. I also lost myself in the horoscope – spending lots of time and money in the occult world finding out about my future and how I could live a better life. But God's hand was always reaching out to me telling me to run to him for safety as the things of this world would be deemed strange.

In my troubled soul I had a dream of God reaching out his hand to me, telling me to come unto him with all my failures and distress and I will find refuge in his presence. Nothing I did changed my life until when one day sitting quietly in my house, I said there is no more running and hiding away from God anymore. Let me find a new life and surrender my will to almighty God who knows the way to heaven's gate. That afternoon I decided to return to the Church because I had stopped going to church as the shame of sin got a hold of my life. I trusted God now fully and have in the last 26 years rededicated my life to his service.

Life has been beautiful since I decided to commit my whole life to him. I am also grateful to the faithful few people who stood by me during my wayward life. And they have been faithfully praying for me to have the duty to come back to the Lord. I give God thanks that he has not dealt with me according to my sins nor rewarded me according to my inequalities but in his mercy and grace got me out of that horrible life of worldly pleasures I was living. All those years I wandered from God I could sense the light of God shining in my soul – He never gave up on me. He was always telling me to come back to him and live a life of faith into his glory. Many are the afflictions of the righteous, but the Lord delivered us all out of them. God's grace has been keeping me going since I decided to follow Jesus. He is the risen and lives. He has saved me and has been a friend to me who sticks closer than a brother. Nothing is too difficult with him. He has made me glad and I rejoice in the knowledge that Christ saves. In fact, I have not chosen him, but he has chosen me and ordained me to be his disciple, sharing the good news of the gospel to the lost and dying world.

I was in the world enjoying the pleasures of sin and God came and let me free from the control of Satan that blinded me and caused me to stray away from the fold of Christ. Jesus promises never to leave me nor forsake me, and I know that when things get difficult, I lean on his everlasting arms and come to him with my burdens and present my request to almighty God in prayer.

I am more determined now than ever before to live a life pleasing a God and I do so with constant prayer. I pray a lot these days even when I am walking down the street. I whisper a pray to God now I have a good relationship with my God and Jesus Christ is the Lord and master in my life. I read the Bible daily and pray every day and now I am really growing in the things of God. Every day is a new day for me, and I live to the best of my ability serving God and be always in his presence. Now I listen to the premier Christian radio station which aids my walk with God in a positive way. I am once again on fire for the Lord, and I do not want to go back to former things of old serving Satan and living in sin.

Jesus reached out to me in my rebellious and stubborn state. He me drew out from the worldly pleasures I once lived for as well as things that would not satisfy. He came into my life and changed me, giving me hope in God and a need to abide by the commandment of God. It is not easy, as Christ himself does not promise me an easy life but with Christ in the world I am always smiling at the storm.

There are times when I feel like giving up, but God has remained faithful, reaching out his hand of love and grace to me and giving me the go ahead to continue in this journey of life.

I am ever so grateful to the Holy Spirit for the work he does in my life. Had it not been for the Holy Spirit who guides me I wonder where I would be today, but praise be to God who understands and encourages me all along the way to glory. There have been times in my life when I felt I was in a dark place with one challenge after another, trying to provide for me and my son, but the light of God has been shining in every dark corner of my experience as I see needs being met and the hand of the Lord guiding me through the decisions I need to take to live a better life.

I had to take a decision on which type of action I would take when I finished secondary school. I prayed like this: 'Lord what would you have me do next in my career.' So, he directed me to pursue a course in Business Studies at the Technical Rush Life Freetown Sierra Leone. I was admitted to the Rush Life and did a two-year course of study where I finished with a certificate in Business Studies, which empowered me to secure a job as an accounts clerk at the West African Examinations Council Freetown Sierra Leone in West Africa. I spent five years there and left on 7th July 1988 for London.

To work was great for me as I was able to earn money for myself after living in poverty growing up as a child. I made lots of friends at work and was able to serve my local community in work. I was always looking forward to payday with gladness that my effort would be rewarded through work because the office was a private organisation not owned by the government. I always got paid at the end of the month, something I always look forward to. My pay packet was the greatest joy I had as I was rewarded for a whole month's hard work serving customers and I was able to provide for me and my son.

Whilst I was looking at options to pursue in my career, I attempted to register at Nyala University but my grade in Maths was not so good, so I was turned down. I then went to train further at the Technical Institute for the Business Studies Certificate course where I passed with flying colours.

When I was working at the West Africa Exams Council I got pregnant and gave birth to Jenner in 1985. His dad was unemployed at that time, so I was left to provide for his needs all alone. Luckily, I had a boss who understood family life and was very easy going in terms of reporting for duty on time as I had to take Jenner to his grandparents' house before going to work and picking him up afterwards.

I had found it difficult to tell my parents that I was pregnant because they were very strict. Having a baby out of wedlock was not the sort of thing they wanted to hear from me, and I was contemplating suicide as I thought of the shame I was bringing upon my family but a friend of mine I was close to was very supportive with me and talked me through the process of breaking the news to my parents. Once the baby was born, my parents were very supportive.

I thank God I was able to share my feelings with someone rather than going down the root of committing suicide for a shameful and sinful action. I wouldn't go to church anymore because of this and I lost some of my friends from there. But I thank God for a second chance to put the record straight to him in prayer confessing my sins and asking him to have mercy and receive me just as I am. But the good Lord remained faithful all through those difficult times in my life. God's voice has been speaking to me in an audible voice saying it does not matter what you have done, I still love you come back to me and continue with the faith of our God. If God had not been in my life at that time I wonder where I would have been at that precise moment. But I thank God that he lifted me up and brought a smile with joy to my face. Now I can see evermore that God has helped me to gain freedom in him. No longer a captive in my own life but freedom, which comes through knowing Jesus, and putting him at the centre of everything I do. There is so much joy and peace in the service of our Lord and I thank God for choosing me to be a part of what he is doing in our day.

John 15 13-14; reminds me of the scripture that says the greater love that a man has for his fellow man the more ready he is to lay down his life for his friends. Jesus has called me friend, so I take him at his word and obey his will in every area of my life. A friend is someone you can confide in when things do not go as planned or when you are faced with obstacles or setbacks. So, I see Jesus as a true friend, and he has also given me his spirit that leads and directs my path. I am very grateful to Jesus because of all the agony he went through to bring salvation to me. It is only love and grace that has brought me safe thus forward.

I know that his grace will lead me onto eternity when I shall see my master Jesus Christ face to face, and he will say well done to his good and faithful servant. Only the joy of the Lord satisfies every longing in my head now. I have fallen in love with Jesus repeatedly and his love is getting sweeter and sweeter as the days go by. My faith in God is seeing me through the challenges of life. I feel closer to God than ever when I am faced with difficulties and I pray for answers to my prayers.

Suicidal thoughts wage my mind even to this day but I try to remain positive and act appropriately and talk to someone I trust about the feelings I am having at that moment and try to seek help from the doctor who increases my medication and afterwards when my moods are normal he brings the dose down again after talking through my feelings. I easily have these suicidal thoughts especially if I am faced with challenges but God has been faithful speaking to me gently to continue to put my trust in him rather than relying on my own understanding of the matter. That is why I pray a lot because when I pray God answers and provides a haven for me to live. This is my problem, the suicidal thoughts, but I am having to overcome these thoughts through prayers and reading God's word drawing strength from the Bible and talking things through to others including seeking help from my doctor.

I have been desperate for a break in life, making me face challenges that seemed hard to overcome but God has been there for me all the way through my life's journey. I always have a second thought, think twice about difficulties and pray for salvation to my problems especially when it is coupled with suicidal thoughts.

Nobody in my family knows about my feelings. I try to keep them to myself for fear of rejection by people who may disagree with my decisions and actions. I am not open to my family about any matter that is worrying to me for fear that they may disapprove of my actions and not be supportive of me through the trials I may be facing and because my parents were strict.

I try to be myself and not compare myself with other people because I am unique, have a creative personality, and can be very adventurous in my daily activities. Life as a mum is not easy, but with the family around me it makes it even more pleasant seeing my child growing up. I tend to hide my feelings from my son as I do not want him to know that I am sad or facing challenges as I think he may not be able to handle the distress very well. So, I try to leave him totally out of it and pray that a salvation is found to my problems very soon. I love my son very much and when I gave birth to him it was the best thing that happened to me – feeling like a mum and sharing blessed moments together. I thank God for the joy he brings to my life and the company we both share together. He was a gift from God.

Chapter 4

What is my purpose for living?

I've always tried to find answers to this question but failed numerous times to get to grips with reality. We are called to this earth for a reason best known to God alone but having said that I am unique, positive, and passionate about life. I tend to take things slowly one step at a time and try to persevere in all endeavours of life. My role here on planet earth is unique. No two days are the same. I try to cope with every area of my life, whether it be family, work, ministry, or relationships with others. I am also very keen to know things and I do this by reprising my knowledge about a given subject matter through social media and reading books. I have also loved my role as a mother and a good citizen. I try to be like Christ, serving my generations in the best way possible. I do make mistakes and can sometimes get things wrong through false judgement but at least I make the effort in trying. Sometimes I give up in doing things if I am faced with setbacks but in other instances, I pick myself up after a few groans and moans to start all over again. Now this is the second time I am taking the opportunity to write my story.

As the saying goes nothing ventured, nothing gained. I do fail as others do but I pick up from there and start all over again. Life is full of challenges and when I give up, I am destined as a failure, but I have learned over the years not to give up as my miracle is on its way.

I learnt self-discipline at an early age. I didn't always tell my parents about my failures and try to deal with matters by myself or if I can't do it alone seek help from friends – family matters a lot to me. I love my family and I thank God that I belong to one and that the good God is keeping us together despite our differences and challenges we face as individuals and as a group of people.

I was not just born into the world – God knew me even before I was born and choose me for such a time as this. I am grateful to God for his unfailing love and care of my life and his daily provision for me and my family. I am here on earth to fulfil God's plan for my life. Nothing is hidden from him, he directs my path and causes me to see myself truly as he sees me. I am very glad that he has saved me for such a time as this, only heaven and God know where I would have been without Jesus.

The decision to follow Christ was gradual as he keeps on speaking to me to come unto him with my whole load of sin and he will have mercy and restore my broken life. I thank God that I took this step to follow Jesus and him alone. The waiting game was over for me only salvation truly matters to my life now. I am saved by the blood of Jesus. It is the best thing I have ever done to know him and make him known to others. God can take me along my path, miracles still happen today, and I am an answer to prayers, therefore I pray that others too living in darkness of sin and shame can be saved. I am passionate about prayer and when I do pray God answers and does what is necessary in the given situation.

When trouble comes my way, I tend to be withdrawn and say very little to others and do deep thinking about the situation in the quest to find a solution but God's hand guides me to pray and when I pray, I feel at ease with myself and a well of joy and peace flows through my heart. I am very homely; my home is where I feel safe, and I thank God that I live in a nice area in London now. I do not like going out except for shopping, visiting or to church.

I am an introvert; I like to have a quiet time to myself with no one to disturb me. I enjoy my quiet moments alone in the house where I can think well and act accordingly to any talk at hand.

Life is not a bed of roses for me. I believe there are times when I must be still in the presence of the Lord and know that he is God. In those moments God speaks to me and shows me his plans for my life. God is in the business of designing a new thing in my life and it will come through and bear fruit. I am waiting patiently for the right time to act in his favour. When I wake up in the mornings, I put the radio on, make a cup of tea and say my prayers asking God to lead me on that day and commit my ways with the Lord. This has been my daily routine and whenever I pray in the morning before doing anything else I feel closer to God and more able to tackle any issues that might spring up that day. I feel a sense of peace in my heart and joy flows through my mind. I have learnt to trust God no matter what the enemy throws my way. He that has brought me safe thus far will lead me onto eternity. I am very privileged to be called a child in God. My heavenly father watches over me and keeps my soul from danger. Satan has no part in my life now.

I take my inspiration from the Lord, therefore before I do anything I should pray and commit to the care of the Lord. God is good, he understands my need and I am blessed to be adopted into his family. God has no grandchildren, so I see myself as a child of God, someone who has love for God and for others.

I am pressing on the upward way, gaining strength daily for living the life God wants me to live. No more struggling just share love and daily in the spirit. I am very much involved in outreach. Evangelism and sharing the good news to the dying world. Prayer has transformed my life for the better and I am now a new person in Christ sharing the good news to the lost and dying world. Whatever I do I am praying, and God has been answering my prayer in a very miraculous way.

Nothing ventured, nothing gained when I pray, the spirit then leads me to take necessary actions on my tasks, and I do see the positive results in a positive manner. I trust in God and depend upon him to see me through life daily. My confidence is being built up to a very high level. No more fear, all things are possible. Just wait upon the Lord for his direction and he opens the doors to me.

I say very little, I am a very good listener. I always give a listening ear to others who have a point or two to share with me whether in a group or one to one.

There is nothing I can't do; nothing is impossible with God. He brightens my journey of life and creates within me a clean heart of service to him and others alike.

When I was 26 years old, I suffered an abortion. I believe God has closed my womb because of that because since then I was not able to have any more children apart from Jenner. This I felt very bad about, and I knew then that life had been taken away from me and all privileges to bear children and be fruitful and multiply had been withdrawn from me. I have since asked God's forgiveness, but I am living with the guilt of terminating a life for existence. What a sad story indeed. When we think we know it all, but God has a way of recreating himself through our hearts and pains. That's my payment for going against God's law. God has a way of disciplining us when we go against his commandment and although he forgives us, and he is a forgiving God, yet the scars of life last a whole life. There is nothing I can do to repair the damage caused but God is merciful and faithful. He says in his Word if we confess our sins he is faithful and just, and forgives us our sins and cleanses us of all sinners.

Life is tough. I have suffered, and every so often been tempted to despair, but I have learnt my lessons and I thank God that I learnt of the Lord's way.

When Jenner was born, I prayed and gave him back to the Lord saying: 'God use him for your glory let him serve you all the days of his life.' And I am still praying for him that he finds faith for himself and follows Christ and him alone.

Sometimes in life we take the wrong road that leads to destruction, but God's love is still consistently pleading with us to move to the narrow roads where there is peace, love and joy in the Holy Spirit. Nothing is permanent on earth; we may all have to die one day and give an account for our stewardship but it is only what's done for Christ that will last. Jesus still saves and he has made me glad through his word. I know I can make it because of God stirring me up to favour and blessings, mercy and forgiveness flows around me and even though it hurts yet this is the root of transformation. God brings me back him. Every tongue shall rejoice in him because he is the God who understands and makes a way where there seemed to be no way.

I have got a lot on my plate now and it is only the grace of God that sees me through from one day to the other. If it had not been for Jesus on my side, where would I be at this moment in time? But I thank God almighty for seeing me through all the challenges, trials, and temptations I go through daily. He is all-sufficient and I have learnt to put my confidence and hope in God alone. Nothing is beyond the realm of God, and I believe I am too far gone yet he sustains me and covers me with his love and care.

Then I must suffer because of sins committed and I feel dirty, lonely, and worn out of his love – I see myself as a castaway from the presence of God but thank God for the calling of the Holy Spirit that matters to my soul in a loud and clear voice saying, 'get up my child and live another day with one'.

I am ever so grateful for his heavenly love and care and know that it does not matter now what I have done, he still loves and cares for me and will be with me until the end. It only takes just a little talk with Jesus to put the matter right. He is all-forgiving and not willing that any should perish but that all should come to repentance. I just trust him for his grace and mercy, only Jesus can fill the longing in my heart.

I've always believed that my story will change for the better and that God will come through for me especially when I pray to God everyday about my needs. I know he is merciful and a wonderful God who desires that I live a life of plenty and do not lack anything in life, but I have to persevere, try harder to get what I want in life.

The journey of life is not cosy but rough with difficulties along the way as Satan is trying call in his power to pull me away from the truth. There are many stones and thistles on my path but Jesus walks close by me every day and he brightens the journey with pure joy and peace. I am so blessed that I know Jesus personally otherwise life would be a wasted journey. There are times in my life when I've asked God for something through prayer, and he has only blessed me with my need without me even knowing about it, but I've still been enjoying the blessings of his provisions especially when I forget that I needed the items and God has already supplied my need. So, it is worth praying and leaving God to answer in his own time. Sometimes I find it harder to step out of my comfort zone and act for fear of failure even though I know that I am doing the right thing. I therefore tend to not have any confidence in myself but when I get active and throw caution to the wind it turns out successful and I ended up rejoicing, knowing that God has brought me safe thus far and he is the one that's leading me on.

Failure is a fact of life for me, but I do not dwell too much on my failure as I see it as a steppingstone to success if I do not give up and keep trying in any given task.

Nothing is impossible with God therefore before a task is carried out, I pray and ask the Lord to direct my path. God has given me the keys to life's journey, and he says, 'use them' and when I believe others will come to the same truth as well, just trust and obey the truth of the gospel and believe in myself in everything I do to the glory of God. I maintain a clear vision and follow my goals daily to secure a well-balanced life where Christ is the centre of my attraction.

I've always wondered why the haves and have nots are in the same category but I know that those who ask for what He offers will receive, while those who don't ask will not receive. To receive one must ask. So, I always ask for help when need be, and offer help to those who God brings along my path.

Being able to think that my existence in the world is not by accident but by God's divine intervention made me think that I have a lot to offer in this world as I pursue my goals in life. I do try to make the most of every opportunity given to me and try to be successful in my role that I am currently serving now in my community – a Christian single lady with one son whom I love very dearly. There have been trials on my journey, but these have shaped me into a very strong person, and it has helped to bring out character within me. No matter what happens I now know that God has knowledge of it all and I try to adjust myself to cope with the demands of the role I serve.

My church family has been very supportive to me in assisting me to put my feet forward in life. I approach the team with a request for prayer, and they have offered prayers on behalf of my needs which I find helpful – knowing that God answers prayers when we call upon him in our distress. If there is a need they supply that according to what is needed at that precise moment. I am grateful that I can be part of the body of Christ in my community and serve God and his people in this way.

I have met quite a lot of people in my time and made lots of friends along the way and the good relationship formed has enabled me to be more confident and active in my society. It is a pleasure to attend church daily and I look forward to worshipping God and also meeting people I care about in my church family and neighbourhood. Through all the trials that I face in life I have learned to trust in God and to depend on the Bible for answers to those dark moments in my life. I know life is not easy and it has not been in my case but one thing I know is that God also holds the future and is carrying me through it all as there are lessons to be learnt.

If I did not have support from the outside world and not belong to a fellowship, I wonder what would have become of me. I may be dead by now, but thanks be to God, who provides us with the basic things that I need in life on those dark moments, I have leaned on Him and see him as the only answer to my problems. I easily get distracted by noise and could not concentrate on the worship if young children are crying all throughout the service. So, I have decided to attend the service that is less noisy with no children around. In my church I attend the 8.30am service and the 6pm service and I try to take notes during the sermon to keep my mind focus so that I can absorb what is being said at the pulpit. It is a way of concentrating deeply on God in that moment as this is the time he wants to minister to my spirit after a busy week. I attend church on Sundays and Bible study where we meet in one of the members houses on a Tuesday morning – term time only. These fellowships have enabled me to grow continually in the Lord and have pointed me deeply to the cross where Christ died for my sins to redeem me from sin and shame. I am so blessed that I can serve God in this way as I feel that I am growing daily in the Lord. He is the reason I live, and I am honoured to be part of what God is doing in my generation.

God is my source of wealth. I approach him as my father in prayer and put my request before his throne in glory and continue in that frame of mind until he answers my prayers and supplies all that I need daily. He has never failed me yet and sometimes it takes a while to get through to Him or even hear

Him speak but still asking God to make his presence known in my life is my most important duty – he hears – his hand is not so short that he cannot save nor his ear so weak that he cannot hear me when I call. The phone line between me and my God is on – Jesus still leads the way to heaven's gate, and I know that I can trust him and only have to obey his quiet voice. It is so sweet to trust in Jesus – just to depend upon his word – he also reveals himself through the Bible which is a guide to my path. His ways are past man's finding out. I cannot fathom the depth of his love. He is all-sufficient, I don't know what I have done to deserve his love. He has loved me with an everlasting love, no one has ever loved me like he has done. I have no other Gods before me. He is the centre of my life, I trust in him. I have lots of disappointments in my life. I don't allow these setbacks to spoil the wonderful love and fellowship I have with my Lord and saviour Jesus Christ.

Going through grief was the order of the day when I lost people who were so dear to me. I try to cope, answering that God knows best in those individuals' cases, although I was very angry with God snatching away my loved ones. I lost my grandparents, my dad, my aunties, uncle and so on. The list goes on but only God knows why he has done this evil to me.

I call this 'Evil' because only God knows the answer to my questions. I try to figure out what in the world these angels of death have got to do with my existence. He gave me a picture that Jesus had to go through death, so death was unavoidable. We will all have to die someday, whether sooner or later and Jesus was the perfect example of death being swallowed up in victory. Now if Jesus was to die then anyone on earth is liable to such cruel death. However, death is not the end for the believer as it is the steppingstone to what lies ahead for us in heaven. I hear of people dying all around me and this causes me to think what on earth is life all about when we must depart from this world in a twinkling of an eye.

Now my mum has lost all her siblings, eight of them and only she survives. It hurts me so much to see them gone away from this world. It makes me think that I do not have to set my affection on things of the earth but to be watchful in prayer looking with Jesus the author and finisher of my faith. If Jesus should go through such injustice at the hands of sinners, I believe I should be prepared to suffer for the sake of the Gospel because God is all-knowing and just.

Now I am living one day at a time with my God, thinking that every day is my last day of living on planet earth because forever living in this world is not guaranteed – even Jesus died and he is my prime example of that kind of story. He lived a decent life on earth but died very young at 33 years of age and only had three years with his disciples during which he taught them about the Christian life.

There were 12 of them in total although one came forward to betray him in the end. After learning the skills of the trade, they were sent out and became apostles preaching the word with boldness through the power of the Holy Spirit. I think I am a sent apostle, sent by my Lord to preach to all nations in my town.

There are many challenges in the journey but my fondest achievement has been bringing the best out of the individual, where I see lives being transformed and people living life to the full with the power of the Holy Spirit controlling their everyday affairs. Only God knows the whole story because minds cannot comprehend what God has in store for me in the future. I take things slowly, one step at a time, with Jesus leading the way. He controls every affair of my life and directs my path.

I am serving the living God, I have denounced the devil and his host. No more turning back. Jesus is holding my hand in his and is leading the way to eternity. I do not fear death anymore as I am now saved by the power of the Holy Spirit – Jesus Christ is my Lord and saviour and no matter what darts evil throws at me I will not be moved by my feelings. I am resting in his everlasting arms. I take God at his word and pray for more of the fullness of Pentecost in my life. I ask God to open my eyes so that I can see what I am supposed to see both physically and spiritually and take actions to come before him in full assurance of the Christian faith.

God tells me not to worry as everything will be alright. It does not matter what I go through now as God oversees everything in my life. No one will do these amazing things for me except God himself through his son Jesus Christ. So, I rest assured that it will all be made plain for me in the sweet by and by. I have so much faith and trust in God that whatever he says he will do what he will do that the father may be glorify in the Son.

To find my place in society is a real struggle as trials are dark at every hand but God is there for me always.

I am a woman of purpose because God's spirit lives with me and guides me to take wise counsel in my everyday life. I am honoured to be a blessing to my generation now and in the future and I am very much stronger now than before. The spirit of God dwells within me and it motivates my heart to his good pleasure.

No more feeling sorry for my lot, just absolute trust in God to see me through one day at a time and commit my days' tasks to him in prayer.

I feel trapped in a vicious circle, but thanks be to God for the breakthrough I found in Jesus. He lifted me out of the miry clay and has established my going every day. I see his hand of love and mercy upon my life, and I thank God for letting me learn things the Lord's way otherwise I would not have known anything of the sort. I would just be dwelling in my sinful way and waiting in this air for a miracle to happen without even the thought of praying. But God understands my needs and has rescued me from the hand of the deceiver. The devil is still deceiving me but now I know which voice to obey and not listen to his lies as he is the father of lies. I am now a new creation, no more living in condemnation.

I have decided to follow Jesus, no turning back. No problem will take me away from the love of Christ which I pursue daily. No matter what happens God is still sitting on the throne of my heart. His love gets sweeter every passing day and I am in a good relationship with my Lord now. The trials and temptations I face are just a steppingstone to being able to discover what God has in store for me. Only if I am patient and wait patiently upon him in prayer, will he reveal himself to me in ways that the tongue cannot describe.

When I need a saviour, friend, I talk to Jesus as he only understands what I am going through – no more tears or fears about the unknown future. Jesus is the way, the maker in life, the promised keeper of my soul. He keeps my soul from destruction so no matter what the enemy thinks I am determined to live for Christ and save him fully in my society. To become part of what God is doing in my world is a great blessing to me. I am even so grateful to God for calling me out of darkness into his wonderful light and for establishing my feet on the rock of Christ to stay forever even though it may not be seen plainly that God is working behind the scenes in my life yet I have the assurance that he is still God and in charge of my life so I rest assured that will make a way for me and that he will award me the victory I need to survive the Lordship of life.

God forgives me when I do earnestly repent of my sins, and he gives me joy in the Holy Spirit to give me the assurance that I am forgiven by my heavenly father and that no condemnation will be in me if I trust and believe that God is capable of forgiving sins if I confess them to him. This I find very rewarding

and true as the devil sometimes brings doubt to my mind causing me to disbelieve in God and his power to forgive sins when
one truly repents of them. I have a relationship now that is based
on trust with God and this assures me also to love and forgive
all those who have sinned against me that I know of. God meets
me at my lowest point in my life and has worked within my soul
to bring me to the place of acceptance and love in Christ and
his work done through me. I have been made in the image of
God, created for such a time as this and I am living life to the
full with God by my side to brighten the journey and assist me
to get the things of life.

Chapter 5

Identity and Love

I tried to get to grips with my existence and wonder where my identity lies. I believe I am on this earth for a purpose which is being fulfilled as the days go by. But where on earth is this identity and for what reason am I here on this earth? I am here to fulfil God's will for my life and contribute to the society in which I belong. I am a black British lady, having been born in London to African parents, so I have a nationality, I am motivated by the desire to succeed in a lot so everywhere I place my hand to do and seek wise counsel concerning the matter that I am dealing with. I throw caution to the wind and take necessary steps to develop myself and others in my team, whether it be at work or at home or in the church setting. I live my life to the full, every step ordered by God and try to be obedient to that still small voice always.

The Lord saves me therefore I am rooted and built up in Christ. He keeps me going and stirs my heart to favour and blessings.

No two days are the same, God strengthens me in all endeavours of my life and takes my hand in his and leads me on this journey of life. I thank God that I have a personal relationship with Christ, and I am a born-again believer. I would therefore describe myself as a child of God born by the spirit of the living God, identified also in Christ. I am redeemed by the blood of the Lamb.

I belong to Christ; he is the reason I live. I am very grateful to God for the Holy Spirit who does his work in my life to bring me to the realisation that nothing is out of reach of God. Whatever transpires in my life is for a reason and that is made clear to me as I seek him through prayer. I am a prayer warrior and like to pray a lot because when I do God answers and gives me comfort in each situation. No matter what I may be going through now God always sustains me and I find that his grace is sufficient to see me through the various challenges I face in my life. I am delivered by the control of the enemy – God has given me victory over the trials and temptations I face, and I pursue my goals and meet with setbacks. His will is made perfect in weakness, and I am so glad to be part of what God is doing in my generation. I know my story and I am reminded that I am dust. God has created me for such a time as this to share my story about how I am getting on in life amidst the difficulties that I face. When I am being discriminated against, I draw courage from the Bible and see my role in his creation and God sees me just as I am and does not discriminate against me for whatever reason. I have been through this evil a lot of times and say that although it hurts me to experience such things in my life yet God sees me for who I am his child that he has saved and redeemed by the blood of the lamb who is bound for heaven and eternal life is being bestowed upon me, so although racism still exists and I do experience such evil I am drawn to the fact that God is in control of the situation and does not let me suffer any loss of my feelings. I have faced racism in every area of my life, but God has always given me the skills to cope with such malpractices towards my life. No matter what the world thinks I know also I am in God's care and am persuaded that God will preserve my life on that great and unstable day.

When I was living in Sierra Leone, I was discriminated against through tribalizing but escaping to London I then realise that I was also discriminated against through strong racism, gender and age. As I get older it is more difficult to secure work because of age discrimination. It hurts me badly but what can I do with people being ignorant about other people's culture? I have a lot to offer to society and therefore persevere in my desire to get the most out of life's chances.

I very much remember turning up for a job interview in London and was told that they wanted a young person. I was gutted left the interview feeling sad that I had just been discriminated against because of my age. These things do happen to me even today. I am living with the need to adjust to all racist and discriminatory behaviour in my world. But I thank God that he does not see me like an aged woman but someone of purpose and that purpose is being fulfilled in my life until eternity when I see my Lord and the saviour Jesus Christ.

I encouraged myself in the world of God as Jesus himself was rejected by many. He came to his own, but they would not receive him, so as a follower of Christ I am expecting that people would reject me also. It's hard and sad to see that this evil is still in our society whether it be direct or indirect discrimination. Only eternity will reveal it all, we just have to wait and see the salvation of our Lord at hand.

Another case I can remember is turning up for a job with British Gas and was discriminated against as they were expecting a white Juliet Smith to turn up. They were very rude to me and told me that they had got their sums all wrong. I left the interview feeling sad and discriminated against. I cannot help it if I am black, that is how I was born. God has created me like this and there is nothing I can do to change it. I live my life to the full as a black lady.

I just don't give up; I keep on pressing on and trying although it takes me longer to secure a job as racism and prejudice plays a great factor to me being accepted for a job. I do persevere and keep on trying repeatedly until I get a good result and my needs are met. It is not easy and has not been an easy road for me trying to live my life to the full. I thank God that I have found a friend in Jesus who satisfied my every need. Although the going is tough yet still, he gives joy and peace and assurance in the spirit of God that no matter what happens he is abundantly able to make all grace abound for me. When this racist behaviour happen to me, I am drawn to the spirit of God and pray that the ignorance is wiped away from our society, that people will learn to accept other cultures as some of us have a lot to offer society.

I now know who I am in God and Jesus is the Lord of my life, stirring me to his divine acts of kindness and preservation of his peace and blessings upon my life. I don't know what I would have done differently with God in my life, but I thank God that I am a believer in the faith as my faith sustains me and makes me grow in the Lord.

No matter what challenges I face God is in charge. He is my God and Jesus is my Lord and master. He is the ultimate sacrifice for my sins. He has saved me and called me out of the darkness of sin into his light. No more straying away from the truth. God is in control, and he is the reason for living. He supplies all my longing and has filled my heart with his love and praise. I have God for the dark moments because I can now see the light at the end of the tunnel. The days of sadness are over for me. I am bursting with joy in the Holy Spirit because I know, and I believe, and I am persuaded that he will keep my soul until eternity. Jesus sacrificed himself for my salvation therefore I believe I must live a life of sacrifice to myself and others that come into my care and deliver a good service to the outside world as I endeavour to pursue the goals that I have created for my life day by day. Life is full of setbacks, but I do not allow these to cloud my vision. I keep my eyes upon the cross and live one day at a time with God being my best friend and companion. I try to serve God and the people God placed in my care in what so little way possible as I know that I will reap the benefit of my actions if I am obedient to the voice of the Holy Spirit and do what is right.

I am motivated by giving because it helps to restore faith in the Lord so that when I give God blesses. If I am able to get more turns for my little gift I do it acutely heartfelt. I like giving especially to the cause of Christ. I am always cheerful when I give to a cause as I get the basic reward openly for my giving. God always multiplies my giving, and this makes me cheerful and filled with joy to know that God is truly in the business of satisfying my needs in return.

I must admit I would like to give more to causes than I give now. I know God sees my heart but resources are just limited to enable me to do so. So, I give the little I can afford and trust that God will multiply. It is the heart that is willing, that God looks at and gives us in return if we do not give grudgingly. God has taught me a lesson, to be a lender and not a borrower. As a borrower is a slave to their debtors. God wants me to be a free citizen helping others less fortunate than myself to make a good life in this world and I am thankful to him for this opportunity.

I thank God for knowledge because with it I can plan and take a stock of my life to see where I am heading to. If successful I rejoice but if faced with failure, I pick myself up again and try again until I succeed. There are many setbacks I face in life but one hurdle after the other has been jumped so that I can now look back and say that God has helped me to overcome my challenges and difficulties.

There is a miracle that happens in my life when I give to help others as God always gives me back in good measure. Sharing together, people have also contributed to my life in ways that have seemed unimaginable and I am so thankful to God for his numerous provisions upon my life. Now I lack nothing as God makes a way for me and supplies all I need for life and Godliness.

I really do have a good relationship with my God that without him in my life would be totally meaningless. I would be dead by now, but he has preserved my life for such a time as this. He opens the way and holds my hand in his and leads me on. I am so thankful to God for his saving grace, if it was not by his Holy Spirit that does work in my life where would I be today.

God through his spirit has created a vacuum in my life which only he can fill. It is not by my own good work that I am surviving the challenges of life but through his love and constant care through me asking the Holy Spirit to come into my life. I can determine to live for Christ always, no matter what I face in life as God sees my struggles and will deliver me from the Lord of the oppressor if I could only just trust and believe in his name. My identity is in Christ, I have been bought with the precious blood of Jesus Christ and now I can say that God is the reason behind my existence. I am committed to serving him all my born days, no matter what I face because I know that he will help me go through in life. The existence I live at is by the grace of God who loves me and sent his only son to die for my sins. I abide in Christ as my ultimate saviour, redeemer and friend. No other friend can be so dear to me like Jesus. God is the answer to all my problems, and I thank God that I am hiding in his wings of love and mercy. No matter what label society throws at me I know that my life is in Christ, my sacrifice and hope.

I am accepted into the family of God, and I am a child of God. He has transformed my life and set me apart for his glory. No one can make me disbelieve that he is the author and finisher of my faith. I am drawn to the need for care and sustenance, and I am also very open to new directions that the Lord may bring along my path. I am so honoured to be part of this system of life and I know that God can see me through the days' tasks if only I have faith and put my confidence in him.

I thank God because the people around me know my standing with God and therefore respect and accept my newfound life in God. I am no longer a slave in the world obeying sinful pleasures but have been set apart for God's glory. The day I accepted Christ was the best thing ever I did for myself and my future because looking back at where Christ found me, I can now say with boldness that my whole life depends on his redemptive work at Calvary. No more fears, no more sorrow, to only believe in God and obey his voice is my duty now. He has set me free from fear and the need to be accepted into the wider society. Sadness and sorrow are all fleeing away – I am living my life for Christ now.

I was drawn into the desire to love and to be loved and have been seeking love through various avenues of life, some very painful and hurtful and I trusted people also who then went onto take advantage of me. My love life has been a roller coaster with very little reward for my effort.

When I give I do it wholeheartedly, giving my feelings to that special person for love but for most of the time I ended up being a victim of abuse and hurt. I had an Uncle Victor Johnson, my aunt's husband who was wealthy and nice. He used his resources to coerce me into believing that he would give me money if only I had sex with him. This sort of behaviour went on for some time. I was always questioning his action towards me as this was not the right way forward, but I was speechless, not being able to do anything to help myself. I was shamed and felt dirty that a member of the family whom I trusted could abuse me in such a way. At the time it all happened I was not financially stable, always finding it hard to make ends meet and to provide for myself and my family. I lost all respect for him and wanted to hide away in a dark place for the guilt of shame I experienced at that time. I was unable to share this evil with my parents at the time because they held him in high esteem and would not believe me. The hurt and pain stayed with me over the years, and I found it difficult to come to Jesus with my feelings. He was a well-respected member of the family and was close to us in every sphere of life and I remained silent in my pain and tried to deal with it in my own way.

Life was tough waking up every day thinking about how painful life was for me in this respect. I had to take a step forward to free myself from the unwanted situation I had myself in. I was no longer in the family home, I had to move house with my sister because of all this because whenever I saw him it brought out past memories into my life. He would threaten me, not to tell anyone about my ordeal and if I did, he would beat me. At that time, physical abuse was the order of the day. Everyone was doing it as a way of discipline so I feared for my life greatly. I was frustrated and depressed with no help at all. I felt suicidal and wanted to take my own life. As I could not bear the guilt anymore and thought that if only I died things would be better for all. At that time there were no authorities I could approach with my problems. There was no one to complain to available. Life was tough with people whom I looked up to taking advantage of my kind nature and abusing me for sexual gain.

There has been cheating in other relationships that I had where my finance was seeing and entering relationships with other women. Thereby hurting my feelings. His name is Samuel Stronge – Jenner's dad. He used to be estranged from me and brought pain and hard feelings to my soul. I feel terrible to have been in such a relationship as I think that he did not love me in the first place. He was dark and handsome, my ideal man but was in love with other women. He was not committed to my love, failing to love me in return and spending time that is precious with me and our son. When I came to London I tried to see if he would come over so that we could spend time together over Christmas, but he was refused entry by the British Government. I felt bad as I was looking forward to his visit.

With Osborne I served as a slave rather than a lover as he was using me to satisfy his selfish desires. I was locked into my own world, so that I could not move up in life. He was verbally abusing me and bringing me down. He never respected me. I don't think he even loved me in the first place. All these relationships ended on a sad note for me. I felt betrayed by people whom I loved dearly but did not love me in return. But there was still hope for me in love when I met Gerston and he has been my best friend ever since we met six years ago.

He has been there for me no matter what. A believer in the faith but although he lives in Freetown at the moment nevertheless he keeps in touch through text. He always tells me that he loves me so much and is missing me. It took a long time for me to finally find love at last but nevertheless I thank God that love reached its hands to me when I needed it most.

Love has really conquered my fears of the unknown, I don't feel trapped anymore since I met Gerston. He was a family friend and we met on Facebook through his friend Olu Williams. He is very loving and understanding. He assures me that he is praying for me always and I believe him. I thank God for bringing us together in love and for finally finding love at last. We hope to tie the knot soon and I can't wait for that time to come.

I came to realise the fact that I could only find love in God. It thrills my heart to know that God moves in my life in such a wonderful way, enabling me to be loved and accepted in this world. God has shown me unconditional love. The love that is sacrificial and I now believe that all these relationships I had were out of greed and selfishness.

Seeking their own needs and putting mine behind theirs, I trusted people so much and as a result suffered loss. God's love is real, true and kind. He is long-suffering and does not seek his own way and all throughout God has been reaching out to me in love and has made me feel accepted into his family once again. I cannot live without him. He is the answer to my prayers, he gives without looking back. He sustains me and now I know I can trust as his love never fails. I depend on God and trust in him for everything. I have gained experience in this journey of life as I have been disappointed several times watching the right treatment from people who ended up abusing or maltreating me. I cannot fathom the depth of his love as he is all I ever needed. He is self-sufficient, always there for me. The Holy Spirit directs my life and now I can say for certain that God is good, he makes a way in the darkest places. He is a shelter in the time of storm when all around me is sinking. He guides and directs my way, and I am so thankful to God for his love and care as I seek to live a life pleasing to him every day. When I take my eyes off Jesus, I tend to sink into my situations but focusing on him alone makes the journey pleasant. God brings people my path now and he tells me to love them unconditionally as he has first loved me, he says do this always so that you may be included in his kingdom at the last day of judgement when Jesus comes to rapture his church.

I try to forgive all those who have caused me grief in my life as I want God to forgive me whenever I sin against him so I pray that God releases his love upon my life and teaches me his ways so that I may enter the heavenly realms of his love. It is only the spirit of God that keeps me going in life because it is not easy especially when I go through these setbacks in my life in a negative way, yet I rely only on his power to establish my goings and bring me to the place where I ought to be with Him. God still cares for me, and He wants the best for my life. I try to trust in his grace and favour and have been motivated to by the need to become all that I can be in Jesus. He is my saviour and Lord.

There is no doubt about it I live my life now through his divine integration and have come to the realisation that he can make all grace abound and see me through one day at a time. No matter what I go through I know that God will give me victory and solve my problems.

I believe in God, and I know that he will see me through any challenges that I may experience. These experiences have shaped my life and have brought out a strong character within me. I am no longer fearful of men and what they can do to me. I only depend on God and take his word seriously in my life. I pray and read my Bible through which I find strength to help in times of need. He is the author and finisher of my faith. I am very privileged to be called the child of the highest God because this is a blessing to me to be heir and joint heir with the father. No greater love can one get from knowing and serving God. He is the Lord and saviour of my life. I am blessed, so blessed to be in his vineyard and I know that he watches over me and is interested in every area of my life.

I came to realise that life is a struggle and only the survivors get it right. One must take every chance given by God to make it otherwise we end up a failure and defeat sinks in. But having come thus far with my God I can now look back and say that God has helped me through the difficulties I face, and he has given me hope again to continue to trust in him for his grace and mercy.

The mercy of the Lord sustains me because God is ever quick to give me forgiveness and blessing whenever I fall short of his glory. He is so good to me; I do not know a lot I can do without him. He is my ultimate sacrificial loins and I know that he will continue to uphold me with his truth. I love the guide I follow daily which is the Bible, and he has been speaking to me throughout my journey. He is God, the one and only being I serve daily. He is the centre of my life. I put him first in everything I do. He motivates me and gives me the reason to get going daily. I have been forgiven whenever I confess my sins to God, and he gives peace beyond all measures to me. He keeps the wheel turning in my life and always keeps me in his love.

The feeling I have towards the opposite sex is genuine. I trusted men in my life and have tried to accommodate their weaknesses but to my detriment. They have since not repented the pain they caused me and instead think that I should suffer in silence. I have released them in my spirit and have since moved on in my life because I want to know more about God and the direction in which he is leading me. I used to take men as a result of these things that happened to me but through the mercy and grace God has worked in my life I have forgiven and been set free from all hurt and pain I suffered.

I now love men more than ever before and see that I am a companion to my other half, Gershon. We talk daily and he is always telling me that he loves me. Something I did not hear from previous men in my life. I am once again loved for who I am and not for what I can bring into the relationship because I have nothing to offer except the love of Christ which constrains me. Not a single day goes by without Gershon telling me that he loves me. He makes me feel like a woman again, finding love in him is the best thing that could have happened to me. I love him so much and know that God will bring us together in holy matrimony soon, where we will be able to live together in peace away from the cares of this world. Gershon is very kind to me and takes me as his sister because he cannot hurt my feelings. He is quick to ask for forgiveness, if by accident he hurts my feelings, and I am also quick to forgive him and move on in life to the next level. We trust each other so much and are keen to be together forever. If I must make a request to God it is that he brings Gershon to London to live with me.

Whatever I want in life, if I ask God he will supply it and grant me my wishes and provide for my needs, because he is a good God. He is all-powerful and a wonderful God, making provisions for his children. So, I take God at his word and pray to him daily for my needs. He knows me through and through and can meet me at the point of my needs. I must only ask him for his daily provision and wait and see the salvation of our God as it draws night. He satisfies every longing in my heart. God is in the business of satisfying my needs according to his heavenly riches. He just wants me to whisper a prayer to him and wait and see him meeting me at the point of my needs. He satisfies and supplies my every need whether it be food, shelter or clothing or the need to be drawn to that special someone in a relationship of trust and care. God is love, in him there is no darkness, the devil goes around tempting me, but God brings resilience to his devices, and I am set free from sin and shame. God loves me, and I am loved by Gershon because he tells me so and I believe him. God has brought us together for such a time as this with six years of courtship, getting to know each other better daily.

Chapter 6

Social Interaction

I have always been keen to be involved in the society in which I believe on a social level as it helps to aid my self-esteem. I am grateful to God for making this possible through various situations of learning and care. The church body helped a great deal in my integration into the wider society. I am also able to get the most out of the chances and see myself getting better in my quest for happy living and able to show positive traits which spring out of my life. I am a good writer, able to get things done at an early stage of life. I am very outgoing and portray a wise counsel of thought in everything I do. I integrate with various people of every culture that is possible and contribute to our ongoing development in life.

I am a church member and I serve my community to the best of my ability. I attend church services every Sunday and belong to the Bible study group which meets in one of the members houses every Tuesday, term time only. I can learn the truth of the Gospel and apply these readings to my everyday life to make me into a better person. I take issues of God seriously and contribute well to the prayers offered by each member of the team of which I am one. I have renounced the devil and all his hosts so now I no longer attend worldly parties or do things that bring the name of God into disrepute, and I am now living a life free from sin and can now say that through the help of God I am what I am, saved, satisfied and rescued by the power of the Holy Spirit which is at work within me.

No more sinning as I am covered by the blood of the Lamb and seek to take the name of Jesus wherever I go. I am saved and know who I am in my God. No weapon formed against me prospers but every figure in judgement is condemned and I take God at his promises' and realise that no matter what darts the enemy throws at one, I am delivered and protected because God shields me in his love and gives grace to help in times of need. I do attend family and friends' occasions where they celebrate birthdays or anniversaries, but I always behave in a good manner in that if Christ was to come back for me that moment, I would be willing and ready to go with him. And I try to be a witness of his love and grace sharing the gospel message to the lost and dying and especially those who are hurting in our society, and I am the messenger of good news declaring the gospel and deliver the word to people especially those who have not come to the faith yet. Most of my interactions is within the family of God where I can attend and take part in worship.

I interact very well in my community, trying to attend social events in my religious setting as I believe that I cannot work together with someone except when we have an agreed purpose, and I must not be unequally forced together with people who do not share my views about the Christian life. I have learnt that when I go out with people who do not love the same faith as I do I tend to be drifted away from the truth of the gospel. I end up living a sinful life that hurts God and the communication line between me and God is cut off. So now it is important for me to stay on the straight and narrow path of the Gospel by applying the scriptures to my daily life: I act on a task and see things through to the end.

I also see a positive result in a given issue I may face, although sometimes I am left with setbacks. However, after trying again and again I then get the desired result I was looking for to a given problem and that brings great joy in my heart, having come to realise that if I can turn things around it will eventually succeed and I am also very happy that finally I arrive at

solutions to my problems after having prayed it through and through. The important thing for me is not to give up but to keep on trying.

There are good people in the church, and I have come to realise that I can trust them with sharing my problems if I need a word of encouragement or an opportunity for prayer. God is putting me close to people who can take my hand in theirs and lead me on the narrow path. God is establishing his will and purpose in my life and now I know that no matter what I may be going through I am surrounded with a whole set of people who would encourage and pray with me. This is a godsend and I do appreciate this in my walk of faith. Therefore, it is important for me that likeminded people who share the same vision stay together to build each other up in the faith. By this we grow up nicely in the Lord and become strong individuals ready to serve God in our fields of life.

I am called to be a witness of the gospel of truth, therefore I am on the lookout for likeminded people who could interact with me to bring out the best out in me. I have always mingled in a church environment as this ensures that I grow up in the Lord and am blessed by hearing the word and putting it into practice to be a better citizen in my community. I am very happy that my church family supports me in this way and are able to pray for me in their quiet moments.

We all need people in our lives to motivate and strengthen us in our time of need and I am glad that I belong to one that caters for my needs and makes me see the true picture of my saved life in the Lord. Jesus is the way, and it is only by following and obeying his command that I can find true happiness in God. To devote myself to this cause I am very grateful and happy to be included into the family of God. God knows me for who I am, and he is very much interested in every area of my life. He gives me courage to step into unknown territory and provides victory over stubborn situations in my life. I am so faithful to his love and care and can say that God has been my helper in all the ages past, a time to sit back and take a view of my life and say, 'Better to have the Lord help me'.

God has been my absolute rock because I never know what I would have become if I had not given him a chance in my life as my life was very difficult. There were lots of hardships along the way and sin got a hold of me for a season, but God reminded me of faith and true to his word he never let me go away from him. He has been there for me through all conditions of life. I am so grateful to him.

I have explored this journey in my life through the contribution of others. I evaluate my life and through my own obedience to do the will of the father. No greater love than this is my ultimate goal as God keeps stirring me on to favour and blessings. I am very happy that God is still interested in my life and wants the best for me always. I must wait upon him in prayer and see the salvation of the Lord at hand. No more delaying teaches only trusting in his love and grace and taking one day at a time with my God.

I am best suited in a team although I can work alone sometimes if the need arises. Working in a team can give me the opportunity to share my opinions with the team members and receive their own thoughts as well on a given matter. I perform well in a team as I can share ideas and exchange views. Teamwork turns me into a better person. We all need people in our lives and being around people sustains me. I learn a lot by interacting because I encounter persons from various walks of life with various levels of experiences to share.

I am quick to learn about something which is of interest to me, and I study and read a lot to increase my knowledge and become aware of my environment, also keeping in touch with what is going on in the world. I do so very actively everyday so that I am not ignorant of things which are happening around me. I like writing and reading, and I enjoy sharing my findings with others I approach. I empower people and share issues that are currently going on in our world. I also receive news from others as to what is happening in our day and nurture those issues in my head to develop my skills further. I sow the seed of kindness and love in my interaction with others. Trying to be the best I can be in every way possible ensures that needs are met fully, and the name of Jesus Christ is revealed to those I come across in my life. I believe my life speaks well and I have been asked by people why I am such a kind and calm person I tell them that Jesus lives in me, and he stirs my life in the way it should. I thank God for being a witness of his love and favour and I can see the hand of God upon life in a positive and refined way.

It takes quite a lot of self-discipline to be where I am now because Satan the devil is always at war with my spirit, but thanks be to God for victory which comes through knowing God and serving him fully. God is love and he has loved me with an everlasting love. He has cared for me since I was born, and I am his child. He has adopted me into his loving care and kind keeping and I am ever so grateful to him for lifting me out of sin and shame and established my going in the Lord.

I thank God that I have someone by me who understands me and is always willing and able to help me through the challenges I face. I am so happy for his unending love that knows no limit. He rescued me from the pit of hell and established my going in him. I am delivered and brought into fellowship with God and the people I interact with they have kept me going. I am honoured and so blessed to be part of this life of quality people who take pleasure in serving God and others alike. I am so blessed and thankful for all that transpired between me and others, able to show a reason for my standing in life through the fellowship I have in God. I know who I am in God, he has saved me and let me be a part of his glory and praise thanks be to God.

I am able in my time of life to love lots of family and friends who are supportive to me in every way. I choose to take and give such warm encouragement in a task that I pursue. If it had not been for people who motivate me and stand with me in prayer where would I be today? But I give God the glory for people in my life and the fact that I am given good advice. There is nothing to me like people in my life who motivate and give me the approval when I am faced with a workload. They brighten the journey in my life and support me in whatsoever way they can. I know I can count on their wise counsel, and I trust them a lot although I don't allow them to take the place of God in my life. I put God first in everything I do and pray for God to help me in my role as a good citizen. I am grateful for the chance to contribute to the society I belong to and know that God will strengthen me and give me the will power to be all I can be in this life of my journey. I am very much grateful and open for new avenues and new things I can pursue now and in the not-too-distant future.

Since I was growing up as a child I have enjoyed being around people because I feel safe and secure when I am with someone. I would sometimes be placed in a dark room alone by my parents as a way of discipline when I had something wrong. A punishment I hated and I would protest very loudly but as I grew older I was able to overcome the fear of the dark room and instead replace it with people around me all the time.

My parents never physically abused me when I was naughty, they sent me into the dark room. That was their way of discipline, and I would cry all along the way.

During my existence I have met with different people bearing various gifts that they have shared with me and I have learned from their experiences and have been able to share mine with them as well. In other words, we learn from each other and develop ourselves in our quests

to be integrated into the wider society. So, I believe that knowing people and sharing in their skills is vital to my interaction and gives me such satisfaction and joy knowing that my needs are met in a positive and refined way.

Chapter 7

Personal Development

I expose myself to literature and digest its content to get the true meaning of life. In the process I have been in an unfortunate situation where I consulted the wrong people to give me an insight into my future life and where I was heading. I consulted the horoscope but realised that the clairvoyants I consulted were asking me for too much money that I could not afford to pay. And their findings on my life were not true because most of the things that they predicted would happen to me never materialised. I was left with no money because of that and feeling let down by people who professed to have the answers to my problems. The sacrifice I was making was outrageous but as in all things I tried but realised that it was getting me further into debt as I had to loan money from sources to finance and pay for my consultations as I did not have very much money at the time. This sort of behaviour went on for quite a few years as they keep telling me to wait and the results that I wanted would happen very soon. My contact with the clairvoyants was well known, and family members who disapproved of me contacting them, but I insisted to the point where it started to lead me to more problems in my life.

I was trapped in a vicious circle, finding the way out was very difficult as I became hooked on following the instructions of one clairvoyant I consulted. There was a turning point for me in that I came to realise that it was all a way of making money for the clairvoyant and I just needed to trust God for my present and future life. I then decided to obey God and take him at his word. That day I decided to turn around was splendid and comforting knowing that all things would eventually work together if I trusted God to lead me and enact his will. With a sincere heart, coming to the Lord was a great joy to ever experience because I had to surrender my will to his and lean on his everlasting hand to take one day at a time to my destiny.

God never fails and I have proved that time and time again. His promises are true and sure as listed in the Bible (his word) for me to follow. Even though I stray from his hand, yet he never gives up on me. The wayward life I was living caused me such problems that I became very depressed and had to stay in hospital. I was admitted to Springfield hospital where I encountered bad treatment from the staff on duty. The doors were locked permanently, and the patients were not allowed to leave the building. I was sectioned and detained under the Mental Health Act as I refused to take medication. The reason for me refusing medication was that I thought at the time that nothing was wrong with me, and the doctor had got his sums all wrong. I was praying a lot, especially in tongues.

I was inspired by the Holy Spirit and they did not understand a lot about what was wrong with me. There was absolutely nothing wrong with me as I communicated with my God through prayer, but the staff did not understand at the time that it was the case. On one occasion I was restrained and put down on the floor and given injections as I refused to take the medication for my wellbeing.

These bouts of sadness continued with me for a while and made me into an angry young lady who threatened to also harm others and myself in the process. I tried to calm myself down and kept asking God to show up in my situation to deliver me from the hurt and pain I suffered in the hands of people who are supposed to seek my interest. In spite of it all the light of God has not ceased from drawing me closer to him. I can always hear the still small voice speaking to me and assuring me of his heavenly love and fatherly goodness.

Despite all the problems I faced I tried to encourage myself as His love is everlasting. He has loved me unconditionally without no limits to the utmost love he shows me.

I'd been looking for pleasures in the wrong places and been through the school of experience before realising that life is too complex to suffer at the hands of failures around me, especially those who do not see things as you do or who are far away in their walk with God. Wild parties did not bring me comfort, but pain and distrust and I can now see that only my faith in God matters to me at this time. Satan is very crafty, he comes in and attacks my mind with issues that he thinks are appealing and makes me do his will, but God's grace has been sufficient to see me through it all. I have learnt in whatever state I am to be content and live my life for Christ alone. Worldliness has left a mark in my life that will not heal even over the years that have gone by. But I thank God for his grace and mercy that I can trust in him and learn from my mistakes. The pain still stands but looking back I can rejoice knowing that God cares and is able to see me through these difficulties that I face.

I thank God that he is interested in my life and seeks to assist me to get the most out of life. The time for mourning about my part is over. I look and rejoice knowing that God is still on the throne, and he is the ultimate sacrificial lamb that was slain for my sins. My sins are too many if I can count them but God who is not in mercy has been my guide and store throughout these days of my existence. I don't have too much in terms of wealth, but I can say that I love the little that I can live on with Christ meeting my every need and supplying all that I have ever needed for life and Godliness. I also lost my home because of being in debt but thanks for the church who stepped in and paid the amount of money I owed. I am ever so grateful to God for providing me with members from my church who support and pray for me and also assist me practically in whatever way that is needed.

Even the Bible says that 'by this shall all men know that you are my disciple if you have love one for another' and I thank God for brotherly love being manifested in my church members. They have chatted with me and helped me out on this journey in whatever way is needed for me to be the best I can be in Jesus. I tried to help myself as I felt ashamed of my problems.

I have experienced a lot of setbacks in my life, and I seek a life free from poverty and lack. I was burgled twice when I was living in Mitcham in 1997 as the thieves broke into my home one day in the evening when I went with my friend Juliana to a prayer meeting. On returning home, I discovered that my home had been broken into and the thieves got away with my possessions. These things took me years to acquire. All my personal possessions were taken away and they broke every area of the house, causing it to be uninhabitable. I had to stay with a friend nearby while I contacted the police and the council about the incident who placed me in a bed and breakfast with my son for 2 weeks. After which time I was given a two-bedroom flat in Wimbledon where I am living until this present time. It was so sad and a difficult time in my life to have to go through such an ordeal, but I thank God that my life was spared and that of my son. We live happily in Wimbledon in peace although Jenner my son has since moved house. He is now living in south Wimbledon. The thieves cleared the house; they took everything. When I moved into my house, I was approached by my next-door neighbour who helped me to get some things. I thank God for their generosity.

Which brings me next to talk about people stealing from my bank account. Stealing my bank card and withdrawing huge sums of money from my bank account. I have indeed suffered loss from thieves, but I thank God that I was spared and am alive to tell my story. It brings back past hurt and pain, but I think that having come out in the open in this way will enable me to address issues that have plagued my life and move forward with God by my side. I have learnt to encourage myself in my God because no matter what has happened, he is still God and is in control of my life. The Bible states that thou shalt not steal yet people steal from each other in such an inhumane way and leave them, including me, feeling very distressed about this evil act.

I have learnt to forgive the thieves who acted in such an inappropriate manner towards me and hope and pray that their peace is withdrawn from them until they repent their evil ways. You can imagine how I felt after this ordeal I felt a sense of worthlessness and powerlessness sweeping over me and felt unsafe, but the authorities have since acted and now I can put the past behind me and move forward in my life with God at the centre of it all.

Friends and family rallied around me, giving me whatever support was needed. I thank God for such wonderful people who helped me get my foot back firmly on the ground because I do not know where I would be today if they had not intervened. All praise and thanks to my heavenly father who sees and watches every action in my life and satisfies every need that I face at that time and even until now. God is still reaching out his hand of love towards me and I know that he will surely see me through whatever the devil throws my way.

I look back and thank God for where he has brought me. He has delivered me from the hands of my enemy and has established my goings. Little did I know that all this was possible with God because he kept silent throughout the ordeal. I said to myself 'But God, I went to a prayer meeting in the church and am only coming to serve you instead. Satan robbed me of my basic things which I spent years to acquire.' The pastor of the church I was attending came on the night of the burglary and prayed for me and encouraged me with words of truth saying 'Don't worry, something big is behind this'. He meant you go to a prayer meeting and your house gets burgled but surely God will see you through this problem.

My life has never been the same. I have changed for the better with God brightening this journey with his favour. I find that I am helped and assisted in all areas of my life where I need to feel God's warmth and God has let people come into my life to assist me to get through the difficulties I face and has set me free from the challenges of life I experience. If God is not in it I wonder what more can Satan do to me, but praise God that he hears the prayer of the righteous. He caused me to blame God for the burglary because how can one go to church and come home to find personal belongings stolen and the house broken into. But I thank God for the Christian friends who stood by me throughout this problem. No better love has a man than people who love and care for others as well.

Now I don't live in fear anymore as God watches over my affairs and has been a shelter in a time of storm when the storms of life wage war. He sustains me and motivates my life to blessings. I have forgiven all these evil people in my life and hope that they had Jesus as a true friend who will lead them to a life of satisfaction in Christ. I hope and pray that they stop sinning and try to earn their living in an honest way.

I eat healthily and try to have a balanced meal daily so that I can grow up looking good and nice and keep fit regularly. I walk one hour a day for 5 days a week. This helps me to stay fit and healthy. I have since maintained a steady weight and I try to do regular exercises on the exercise bike from time to time. This has helped me maintain a positive outlook in life.

I eat 3 times a day with breakfast, lunch, and dinner with small portions. This helps in my own personal development body wise. I see my dentist twice a year to service my teeth and the last time I visited her she complained that my teeth are all falling out. I wonder why this is the case as I think they are glued to my gums. But having said that physically I have no health problems now just a frequent knee pain which is slowing easing down.

I am blessed to have family and friends who contact me to find out what going on in my life. When the weather gets cold they wonder if I am managing to keep warm. I appreciate the various people in my life who see that things go well and I am thankful to God for blessing me with people who have such love and affection.

Chapter 8

Raging Storm

The most distressing incident that happened to me was when my dad died suddenly from a heart attack in 1993. He was living in Sierra Leone and was due to visit me in London that summertime when this sad incident happened. I was devastated and wondered where God was in all this. My father woke up on the morning of the 24th of January 1993 and was about to have his bath when suddenly he became ill and was rushed to hospital, but unfortunately he passed away after a few minutes. He had also been suffering from his blood pressure, a condition which was unknown to him while he was still alive. It took me a lot of time to grieve as I was a special child to him, and he died on Jenner's birthday, which makes it worse for me. I wondered where God was in all this as I was so deeply saddened about the whole affair. God still cares and he understands my pain so much more and I was also blessed by the comfort I receive individually by the Holy Spirit and from other friends who share in my grief. Dad never had favourites, he loved all his children equally and gave us all the time and resources available to him while he was living upon the earth. He was a very social man, always bringing laughter to everyone he was in touch with.

Throughout all the grief and sadness that I suffered through the loss of loved ones I have also trusted in God because he knows best, and his ways are real as he keeps me safe in his everlasting arms.

I will never forget the time God reached out his hands towards me and took me by the hand and led me on the way to righteousness, holiness and Godliness. These situations have formed a seal on my life and cause me to be closer and closer to the

Lord. Every day he fills my life with his faith and blessings. There was no one to act like a dad anymore as my beloved died and was taken away from me at such a very early stage in my life. It left a vacuum in my life which only his grace can fill and God has been filling my life with his blessings and endurance. I have been able to stick with God through these tough moments though grief and sadness and I can say now that the Lord is good to those who fear and love him. The thoughts of missing my dad still wage war with me as I always remember and celebrate in silence his anniversaries whether it is his birthday or his death anniversary. I have since lost many relatives in and have learned to cope very well now with grief and sorrow. God has been comforting me in my mourning for my lost loved ones that I cared for greatly.

The death rate in Sierra Leone is very high, lots of people there die prematurely due to no fault of their own. There is no money going around to pay for medical help so only those who can afford it are able to seek medical aid. The medical team can only treat a sick person if they can afford to pay. This is so sad as most of the people just cannot afford to pay for medical care and rely on donations from others to fulfil that role of providing money for the medical care. Thank God for the NHS here in London and the fact that we can all have good medical care if we fall ill, and they are perfect in their work and give us good care.

My parents also had to seek a scholarship for me to study at the Methodist girl's high school. I was awarded a scholarship by the city council when I got to secondary school. I did very well in school and graduated with 5 GCSE's 'O' levels in 1979. Learning for me was great fun I enjoyed my school days although they were sometimes not the happiest as when I fall short of standards, I was corrected through discipline by my teachers, something I always hated. I never failed in school and always got the top grades. There were some teachers who left a lasting impression on me.

I will never forget their kindness to me and the interest they showed to me. Some of them have since died and that brings sorrow and sadness to my soul but I thank God that I had most of the learning I was supposed to get through their teachings. There have been times when I needed to take stock of my life and see how far God had brought me and thank God that no matter what happened to me, I will always honour and serve and because he is all that I have ever wanted in my life. The pressure of life is getting to me as I sometimes feel stressed by challenges but when I have turned to God in prayers, he has lifted the load I have been carrying and filled my heart with peace. He also gives me grace to continue trusting and abiding in his love.

I came to realise that the battles that I face daily are not my battles but the Lord's, therefore I yield myself to God and commit my ways to him because he knows best and will direct my actions according to his word. Therefore, the word of Christ is essential to my everyday needs. I read it, digest it and act upon it to give me hope and a future. The spirit of God keeps me going. I abide in his love. Therefore, whatever storm I face I am persuaded that God is there with me all the way through reaching out in love and care to my situation and giving me peace.

I've always been a quiet and reserved woman so whenever I am faced with problems I am easily drawn into my own world and tend to reflect on why such problems have occurred in the first place. I don't stop to think that I can pray and ask God to solve it instead feeling sorry for my lot and putting the blame on the circumstances I may be facing at the time. I turn to pray at the last resort after talking my situations through with family and friends who care about me. I am conservative in my nature, looking only to God to bring it to pass in my life having prayed it through.

My desire to pray is because I can now say that I have a good relationship with Jesus, and I have been able to accept his love and care in my life because over the years I have trusted in his unfailing love and provisions for my life. He has been a good, kind, and faithful God to me no matter how many times I have abandoned his directions. The revelation I have about God is because I am his child, and his spirit abides within me guiding and protecting me from all evil. I am blessed to be alive to see this day and I take one day at a time with my God who is the ultimate sacrifice for my sins.

I like my quiet moments in which I spend time on my own meditating on scriptures and praying to God for my needs and the needs of others. I try to concentrate well on a task and get the it done in each space of time. Life is very rewarding for me as I believe I have achieved so much in the years I have existed on earth ploughing through the precious years that God gives me I discovered some value of truths about myself and what I can achieve.

I am a law-abiding citizen, always obeying the rules of the Lord. I enjoy cooking, listening to the radio to my Christian stations as I find the healing on the radio very inspiring and that aids my ability to be successful in my Christian life. I thank God for the few people in my life now who support me and give me the chance to make a good head start in my life. They have been very supportive and understanding to my needs and welfare. I tend to struggle a lot in work as I do have little jobs here and there and find it difficult to keep hold of a job for a long time. This is because I am living in a racist world and people tend to discriminate a lot against me whenever I apply for a job. This is what makes life tough and difficult because I lack the resources to live a good life.

There have been blockages in my life especially in my finances as I always find it hard to make ends meet. I fear the end of the month so much so that I ended up having headaches frequently as I am thinking about how I will be able to pay my bills at the end of the month.

The work I do, and the money is not making enough income for me to be able to live a more prosperous and successful life. I am struggling to make this happen. But I know that one day if only I continue praying and asking God to provide, he will open the way to his heavenly riches whereby I will be able to get the amount of money I need to live on with the little I have coming in every month. I try to give to charity and charity people that come along my way. My greatest need is to see my future life blossom with the aroma of God. I know God can provide for my needs and I am trusting in his favour to bring it to pass in my life.

I fear answering the phone when I am overdue payment on my bills. But having said that God will surely and very soon work it all out for my God. I await his divine intervention in this matter. That's why I believe in God's word as it is powerful and can change my life for the better.

I always like to help where there is a need that has been brought to my attention and contribute in a little way as the spirit leads. So, where there is an appeal on the radio, I give to a just cause so that others too may benefit from the services I received when it be much or less. I am generous in my giving and have a clean heart which other people have commented on. I thank God that it's only his grace that keeps me on the narrow path. I am not perfect, still falling short of God's glory, but his mercy and love reaches out to me, so I bless the name of Jesus for touching me worthy of celebrating in the good news of the gospel. It is better for me to give than receive because God loves a cheerful giver. I don't give out of obligation but out of love for my fellow human beings knowing that God will reward me so much more if I do not give up hope. I enjoy being around people sometimes as it helps my self-esteem a lot and gives me the assurance that I am not alone and that others do care about me. I tend to take pleasure in other people's affairs and try to be supportive to them as best as I can. We all need that push from time to time to bring out the best in us by people who take pleasure in our wellbeing. I am happy to serve others.

Sometime in August I was running to exercise my body as I need to control my weight to its required standard and keep fit. I suddenly injured my knee; I was unable to walk for over 18 weeks, going to the doctor who prescribed medication for me, and he also referred me to physio sessions. I followed through with those sessions successfully and finally made a recovery. I thank God that through the days I found it difficult to walk I was not bitter to God about the whole incident. Instead, it was very positive knowing that one day I would be able to walk without feeling any more pain and God has not failed me in that request. Now I can walk freely and without suffering pain any more. I was unable to travel a far distance for over that length of time, but praise be to God who healed my knee and now I can use it fully today, doing one hour of walking every day for 5 days a week.

Jesus has been my Jehovah Rapha. He has healed me and now I am free from pain and all discomfort that I experienced while being unwell. I also give thanks to family and friends who stood by me during my process of recovery from illness. I am very glad now that my knee is no longer in pain.

My life is filled up with various challenges, some big, some small but God has been at the heart of it all. I confess my failures but also say that God has given me the chance to stand up again on my feet and move forward in the desire to find happiness and satisfaction in life. My life is not all that cosy but very rocky and stiff, however I have discovered that when I invite God into my life he comes in and does what is necessary in my development. He has blessed my life with people who want to see me successful in life although some others have also been jealous of my achievement in recent years, but I have learned not to worry but to focus on the future and live one day at a time.

I thank God that I can call upon him when troubles come my way and he responds to my need and gives me the solutions to any difficulties that I may be facing at that moment. My life is busy, but I try to live quietly away from the difficulties of life. I spend much of my time indoors depending on the weather of the day. If it is nice and sunny, I go for a walk in the park meditating on God's creation and the need to be part of what God is doing in our world. I am very privileged to live near the common.

Sometimes I wonder how I could survive the challenges life throws at me as I make a way through life's struggles. But having a little faith in my God has been the source of my victory. God has always helped me put my foot forward and claim victory in every area of my life. The day's tasks seem mundane but praise God that I have a God who cares and understands my struggles. I put everything to God in prayer and wait patiently for answers to my requests. He has never failed me yet; I trust in him for his wonderful love and guidance. I have witnessed his divine love and mercy upon my life and have come to realise the fact that one must trust the Lord Almighty and fully to see the greatness of God upon one's life as these challenges can be very hard to cope with.

The good Lord has showed me mercy on various occasions as I am only human and at risk of sinning all the time, but he has been quick to forgive me for my sins and lifted me out of the pit of sin, death, and hell. I found out for myself that the journey of life + is a rocky one but his favour, and goodness with long suffering has paved my journey to his divine intervention. I have failed God many times and decided to obey Satan's rewards rather than God's, but he has not given up on me and he keeps assuring me of his love and mercy.

The race is not for the swift, neither the battle for the strong but through all other options available to me God has caused me to take the right step to eternal life and has motivated me to create a fulfilled life in his presence. At heart I could say that God is the ultimate reason behind my existence because he knew me even before I was born and ordained me to blessings in his vineyard.

I am so glad that he has set me apart today for his pleasure which is to worship God in the beauty of his holiness. That comes from all angles of life, but his grace is sufficient to see me through one day at a time.

Sometimes I am overwhelmed by fear, but perfect love cast out fears and I thank God that his love is perfect in my life. He has loved me unconditionally and I am very grateful to him for this. I have made bad choices in life and have failed in my quest for development, but God has lifted my head above my circumstances and has given me hope to trust in him alone. Sometimes I feel that I bother people a lot with my problems and the difficulties I face as I am aware that they too have got their own problems to solve but they have still been able to listen to my complaints and give me wise counsel in the matter I am dealing with.

My God is behind my existence on planet earth, he sees me through life's struggle and gives me victory in every situation that may hinder my development. I am grateful to God for the opportunity given to me to serve and be of service to others. It is only by his grace that I am what I am. I am only a kind-hearted individual who seeks to serve my community in whatsoever spheres of life I find myself in. Today is a great day for me as I take every moment seriously and encounter the divine nature of God in my everyday life.

Tomorrow will be another new day in my existence but now I am only living for today and thank God for the opportunity to be alive to see this day in the land of the living.

I believe God exists and that he is watching over me day and night to fulfil his purpose and will in my life. I have never doubted the reality of my relationship with God. I trust in his unfailing love and realise that I cannot do it alone. I needed a saviour to help me to the end, therefore I decided to accept Jesus into my life and make him Lord of all. I have truly known the faith that lies within me fully and participate in his fellowship.

However, the journey has not been smooth as Satan seeks to destroy my existence due to constant sinning against the will of the father. I feel unable in those situations to resist the devil and instead obey his voice instead of the Holy Spirit and therefore come to sin against God. But God has been merciful to me and has caused me to repent and turn away from sin and selfish behaviours. God has helped me to overcome the obstacles and the challenges that cause me a lot of social problems that involves lack as well.

I am all-sufficient as my needs are being met as the days go by through answered prayers. I enjoy praying and putting my request to God and wait to see him move on my behalf. He has been showing me favour and has blessed me with good things that we all take for granted. It is not easy waiting for God to move but when I persevere, he comes through for me and grants my wishes and also supplies my needs. I had a problem which in my eyes was difficult but with God he made all things plain to me and gave me victory over the trials that I faced at that time.

About 5 years ago, I accompanied 2 people to the bank to withdraw cash from their accounts. They then turned around to say that I have stolen their money and called in the police, but I was so surprised at this allegation and decided to pray about this. I was questioned at the police station about this but after days of deliberation I was acquitted saying that they had not got sufficient evidence to bring a case of theft against me. Can you imagine a child of God like me who found God and all areas of my life + being accused of theft? I prayed and asked that the truth be made known, and I was set free from all charges. This is absolutely the work of God as he gave me favour at the time at a very difficult moment.

I have since found faith before God and man ever since I am faced with problems. He has vowed never to leave me nor forsake me, and I have taken his hand of love and peace upon my life. Through all, I have learned to take God at his word and depend solely upon him. People are wicked, they just see your kindness and decide to get you into trouble, but God is the one who sets the captives free, so I thank him that he has delivered me from the hands of people who are considered my enemies. In my situation, no weapon shall prosper.

I am a free born citizen one who is free to live a life from the trials and tribulations that society throws upon me. I am committed to making sure that the love of Jesus is preserved upon my life, and that of others especially the people I love and care about. Trials come and go and it's only the love of Christ that constrains me and leaves me to be brave and strong in him.

As a woman of purpose, I must admit to sometimes not believing that God can see me through the struggles I face. Sometimes since Satan works on my mind and tells me negative things to do but God's love enables me to take a positive step and act appropriately to discover my purpose in life. I have had pain and setbacks in my life, and these have formed the basis of me getting to the next level in my walk with God. He has comforted me when I am distressed and given me a blanket of warmth when I am cold and weary. I cannot live without God. He satisfies and says, 'well done' and has given me grace to help in time of need. I am very happy to be living in Christ now as he is all I ever wanted. He reaches out is hand towards me in love.

I have trained my mind to pray like this, asking God to create in me a clean heart and renew a right spirit within me. This form of prayer is being read daily and I also thank God that he has been answering my prayers as other people I interact with see that I have a pure and clean heart. Whenever someone commends me for this, I give God glory because he makes this possible and grants my request in prayer. So, when people gang up against me and make false allegations of theft against me, I always pray and ask the Lord to come and take control of the situation and give me peace and joy in the Holy Spirit.

There are some people out there in the world who act out of malice and hatred towards me and I consider them my enemies but having discovered them not to see things in a positive way. I tend to ask God to have mercy upon them and lead them to repent and turn away from their wicked ways and live a life of blessings and hope in the Lord. I am committed to forgive and I have also learned to forgive all those who do me wrong. God wants that for me, and I am happy to obey his voice.

Prayer is when I talk to God and tell him about how I am feeling daily and ask for things that I need to live a comfortable life. I have been fortunate to be a prayer warrior in my community particularly being involved daily in praying for people who are sick or are suffering from diseases that endanger their lives.

On Thursday lunchtimes I take part in prayer over the radio station Premier Christian radio and pray for people who are suffering from illness. I have been able to hear about how God has healed people that I pray for over the radio and how he has given new life and meaning to those hurting in our society.

God has restored broken lives in our land, and I am happy to be part of what God is doing around the world. Prayer leaves no distance to God as he can reach us wherever we are. Lives have been healed through the disciple's intervention of God upon our lives and the faithful support of those who are praying. I am an intercessor in the body of Christ, always praying for the need of our society to blame and God has been answering my prayers in his time. He gives wisdom and the will to call upon him in every area of life. So, if there is a prayer needed or something you want God to do in your life just let me know and I will present the request to God in prayer and trust him to do the impossible in our day.

No request is too big for God to solve. He has answered my prayers in times past and will continue to do so in the future; only believe all things are possible with God. Prayer is the central part of my life because it is like a suit you put on and off, when you don't need it, it opens the way to heaven's gate and the communication line actively seeks a continuous flow of current. When I pray to him it doesn't matter where I am now in my relationship with God because God takes me from my point of contact to take me by the hand and lead me to the way everlasting.

I am happy to serve in this ministry of interceding for the needs of people in our world and pray for God to move and solve every problem that we may have in our world. This gives me great joy to see people happy in themselves knowing that they have been blessed with good things and in good health after a brief spell of sickness. I still believe that I have healing hands and can pray for others who are sick and see them recover from their sickness. God can see us through these dreadful things that eat us up.

God in his mercy has saved me and given me a mission to pray for the world to come to the knowledge of his saving grace and set free from sin and sickness.

I am so glad to be part of what God is doing in our world and for the opportunity to take an active role in meeting the needs of myself and that of others and be able to witness positive results from my encounter with people and the world. I bless God for the ministry of intercession and to become a prayer warrior presenting needs of others to him in prayer and thanksgiving. God has opened my eyes to the gospel truth, and I am also willing to pray that others experience the same too and be part of what God is doing in our world.

The times are swiftly flying by, and it takes a lot of courage and willingness to be part of God's development as we seek to serve others and God. Sometimes life could be full of sabotage with lots of problems along the way since we live in a very unstable world where there are lots of challenges that can knock us off track, but God is in control of my life and motivates me to keep holding onto him no matter what I may be facing as he is in charge of my life and will surely see me through it all.

Chapter 9

Possibilities of Life

I have always been seeking a way forward in life, operating on a given talk and reaping the rewards of my actions making a positive stand in the quest for a great life.

There have been times when things have not gone according to plan and I tend to question my actions but my little faith, that inner voice within, tells me to pursue the matter further and not to give up on my dreams. This is true for the season I am living in now as there are problems and things to sort out that do not always lead the way to recovery.

Nothing is impossible with God; I keep telling myself when faced with a hard problem which I cannot solve by myself. Therefore, I seek the counsel of others I trust to throw on the situation. I then digest the reformation and pray over it asking God to receive one rightly to take the most appropriate action. I have surrendered my life to God in kind keeping and I feel blessed that he has adopted me into his family and called me his child. As I no longer have a dad, I look to God as my heavenly father, consulting him in various spheres of life and communicating my plans to him in prayer, asking him to lead me in the right path I should take. He gives me all, my helper the Holy Spirit, to guide and ready me in all truths.

I have a blessed relationship with my heavenly father as he is always by my side when I need it, whether in the good times or in the bad times. He is a very good and caring father, one I can always count on in my daily life. He senses when I am happy or sad and when I need that special someone to chat with and I trust to give my closest attention as I have and whisper a prayer to him in confidence and he answers to my need. He is just very close and dear to me, more than words can express. I am so happy to be in a good relationship with him as I have come a long way through various challenges that I have faced. He has loved me unconditionally and has never failed me yet nor forsaken me. Even though I wander from his hand I get that still small voice always to cheer me on to come back and say to me that all will be fine. It does not matter what I have been going through in life, he sees and understands. My heavenly father can be there for me twenty hours a day, whenever I need someone to talk to he is always there. I can always look to him for everything and approach him in prayer concerning my needs and wishes. He cares for me so much.

Nothing is hidden from him; he knows me through and through and has been my source of joy on this earth that I am living now. He understands and is the God who directs and orders my step according in his will.

I have learned to trust in him and bring my petitions before his throne of grace. I don't know what I can do without him as he is all I ever wanted in life. He is the sacrificial loins that were slain for my redemption and God sent Jesus to pay for my sins, a helper in time of need.

When I lost my dad, I thought that the whole world was against me as he was the most loving and caring person in my life that I had ever known. I have lived with him all throughout my life and thought kind and nice things about him, but when this happened, I believe God was teaching me a lesson not to put my trust in humans as they are around us for a season but soon they will fade away and be called to glory. I then tried all other things that can fill the space created in my life. Entering relationships that have been abusive and so on but when I turned to God himself the hurt and pain suffered suddenly went away and I feel safe and secure once more in love.

For me my heavenly father's love is greater than anything I can get out of life. He is just too good to me. Words cannot express my feelings and appreciation for him for all that he has done for me and is still doing in this season of my life. He is all I ever needed and all I want for life and Godliness. He makes all things beautiful for me in his time. He gives me praise to trust me during the difficult moments of my life and has been my absolute rock.

I can now lean on his everlasting arms, he is the answer to my prayers because when my dad died, I cried out to God to provide me with someone who could satisfy the need of a father to me. I tried various people who turned against me and misused the trust I put in them until when I finally surrendered any will to him. He says to me look no further afield as I can meet the need in your life and since I decided to trust and put my confidence in him, he has never failed me yet. I put my hope in his word and read the Bible where he reveals himself and his nature to me. I enter communication with my heavenly father daily, seeking which direction I should take, and he leads me by giving me prompts to my spirit through the guidance of the Holy Spirit. His direction is perfect as I always come up with the right course of action to take on a given issue that I intend to pursue for that day. You will agree with me that Satan too is trying his own with me by counteracting God's lead and saying what is not wrong on a given matter, but God gives me wisdom to determine the best way forward to doing the thing I intend to do daily.

He understands where I am coming from, a sinner, condemned and doomed for hell but he has made a provision for me to return to him with arms open wide entering his presence with boldness through the intervention of Jesus Christ, his son, who paid the penalty of sin I owed due to my sinful nature. I will never forget God and all he is doing in my life today and I am always grateful to be included in the number of those whom he has called out of this dark world of sin. I truly appreciate his care and kind keeping upon my life; whenever I need that special someone to talk to, he always there giving a listening ear to my needs and hearing me out.

I came to realise that everything is possible with God by your side if you have faith. A little faith is enough to see me through the problems I face. God is someone I can trust and take at his word that whatsoever he says he will do what he will do, and I have learnt over the years to confide in him everything that disturb me whether little or big. He is the person I can be able to say loving things about because he has been there for me throughout my life and is holding my hand in his and leading the way. I always learn to be a source of his witness to others' lives as the spirit leads and directs me.

I take charge of every opportunity offered to me to make things happen as the spirit tends to bring joy and satisfaction to my life and that of others. I have learned the hard way going about in my selfish and wicked ways, but the spirit of God has motivated my mind to keep on the straight and narrow path that leads to a well-deserved life in his presence. God comforts me with all the comfort that I can get at the time of mourning because it took me a few years mourning the death of my father.

No two days are the same with God, as every day is a new day facing new challenges and seeing God work it all out for my good in a new way. Trials come and go, and I am made stronger in my character and have trusted God throughout the whole ordeal of my trials. God has set me free, given me a new lease of life and stability.

Now I am so assured of his presence and divine intervention that nothing can take me away from his arms. I am resting perfectly well in his bosom and can now see the salvation of God at hand in my life and wellbeing. Everything I want is possible with God, I duly just must ask, and it will be given unto me.

I am asking daily in prayer for his will to be done upon my life as it is in heaven and pray that the kingdom of God comes on earth always. I am responsible for the actions I take in life therefore I pray and ask God to help me take the right decisions so that I do not end up regretting it. God sealed my life with favour and blessings from heaven; he has given me all I need in life, and I am thankful to him for this.

When the sense of hopelessness kicks in God lifts a standard against the enemy and gives me peace to trust in him fully because although things are going well for me now yet shall Satan be still after my joy, trying to steal the blessings God has reserved for me, so I must not give him any chance to wage his wicked way in my life. I try with the help of the Holy Spirit to seize every chance given to me by God to live a rewarding and fulfilling life and wait upon him in prayer for direction. God has been in the position with me to lead and confront my life to the full. He is the only one I serve daily. I do not put things or other humans in my life to take the place of God in my walk with him. He is all and in all to me. He satisfies my longing and controls every area of my life. Therefore, I am at peace with God through the Lord Jesus Christ and I live to serve him daily. I entered this relationship with God ever since I was born.

Not knowing where my life will lead me and having gone through various challenges in life that sort me out and enable me to be fit and able to serve God fully.

I have been bought with the precious price of Jesus' blood at Calvary. He is all I ever needed. He satisfies my every need and has been my shelter in those trying moments where I feel I cannot go on any further. He keeps on telling me to persevere and not give up as my miracle is on its way. I have faith in God and what he can do if duly I believe in him and trust him daily for needs. He gives me food, shelter, and clothing for these provisions in life I say thanks father because you have showed me that you care for my needs and all that I do for life and Godliness.

The situations I am faced with are only temporary as God can change things for me and turn it around so that the glory goes to him. I take him at his word and look to the author of my faith for the next step forward. Only Jesus can satisfy the longing in my heart. He instigates my every move for his purpose. I am very glad to be part of what he is doing in our world to bring hope and deliverance to those around my whom I serve daily.

I am at a good standing with God currently in history because he is the one who drives me to favour and honour. therefore I have confidence in him.

I only need to pray and call upon the heavenly God to grant my needs and he has meets them according to his riches in glory. My God is a wealthy God who can supply all I ever wanted or need in life therefore I only must pray and call upon him and he will meet me at the point of my need. He supplies all my needs fully to my satisfaction. Nothing lacking. He is just the perfect friend I have these days when there are deceitful people around. I comfort myself in his care and keep and ask him to take control of every situation that has troubled my mind. He has been granting my wishes and making a way for me in the wilderness of faith.

I may be alone in the house but don't feel lonely as Jesus' love is all around me wherever I go, and he is with me wherever I am. But having said that only sin in the ways make me feel lonely as the communication line is broken between me and God but once having repented I am reinstated once again into fellowship with my Lord and saviour Jesus Christ God and the Holy Spirit. For this reason I always make it a point of duty daily to repent of any known or unknown sin so as to be in fellowship with God.

I came to know that God does everything beautifully in his time, therefore the timing of God is important in my request for him to provide and help me in this life. I have come to the realisation that when God takes the driving seat in my life no evil will come near me, and I will be full of hope for the future. This is a something in my life as I consider letting go of all my fears and rely solely on his doings to see me to the end of time. The waiting is long sometimes and causes frustrations on my part as I may be suffering from the lack of intervention which is crucial to my wellbeing but waiting patiently for God's time is so great as he does everything perfectly.

God has been taking me through the school of experience and teaches me how I need to trust and wait upon him for my provision and divine intervention. This may be hard sometimes as I needed a quick answer to a given problem that I may be experiencing at that moment. Trusting in God can also be a bit shaky sometimes, but I must rely on him and tell him to have his own way into my life as his promises are true and perfect and his timing for me is also very good.

Pain is something God uses in my life to build me up for his glory because when I am in pain, I learn to lean on him and pray a lot that this pain should go away and that the Lord should also set me free from sufferings.
When I am sick and suffering from pain, I learn to trust God more and also pray a lot that his thorn in the flesh should die down and also pray that God releases me from the sufferings and discomfort I am suffering from. At some time in the past, I have suffered from regular pain causing walking to be a problem. I then travel not far and because of this only travel with public transport and go short distances. I keep travelling within the Wimbledon area where I live.

I further discovered that this pain lasted 18 weeks. A very long time to groan and moan about my situation. But having said this

I was able to seek God more, pray more for my healing whilst taking my motivation to make me better. During my pain, he trained me up and gave me the power to come before him at the altar of prayer daily and be taught in the school of experience where I derived a certain trust of myself.

God has used suffering and pain through sickness to bring me closer to him. The waiting is tough, but God has been giving me grace to follow which has been sufficient for my needs. The pain can be severe at times, and I suffer a lot of discomfort but one thing I know is that God is always in the middle of my suffering and pain.

I have been in a dark place through pain and suffering and I have also learned the hard way, that is to keep on believing and trusting God to soon deliver me and come to my aid in this struggle to have a body that is free from suffering and pain. I look up to God in my lonely hours, especially at night when the pain is so severe that it sometimes stops me from sleeping at all. I am always left with God by my side, wondering when my breakthrough will come so that I can be healed and set free from this suffering that plagued my life.

I sometimes marvel at the way God works as I see his hand reaching out to me in love and also how his caring disposition has been bestowed upon me in my hour of need. Suffering is hard and one can agree with me that no one wants to be in pain of any sort whether in sickness or otherwise, but God brings these situations to test my faith. And my faith has been tested very well in that I have not murmured or complained but put my confidence in God to see me through it all. He is the God who cares, and I know that he loves as well therefore I keep my hopes alive in him and trust him to see me through one day to another in my time of need.

Sometimes when I pray about my suffering in sickness, I don't have an answer to my prayer straight away. I then ask God for mercy and repent though probably there is sin in my life. After having confessed my sins, I have peace in my spirit and assurance knowing that God has forgiven me for all known and unknown sins and if I need to make amends to anyone I further approach them and ask for mercy; then I continue in an attitude of prayer for a further time presenting my request for healing to God and actually I sometimes forget that I was in pain after being healed and enjoying the blessings of my healing.

My mind therefore wonders onto various other things which are relevant to me at that time and I totally forget to thank God and render my praises for his healing hand upon my life. I am only human, these things do happen. I don't want to be ungrateful to God for healing me and not offering a prayer of thanksgiving to him for his divine healing upon my life. I therefore need to show politeness and gratitude to God for what he has done for me in healing me and setting me free from pain and suffering. I feel bad sometimes after having been created I then forget to offer a prayer of thanks to God for the healing I receive from him. I tried to keep up with the busy schedule that I love to do.

Even up to now I sometimes have a pain in my leg and foot and can't walk very well. I enjoy walking a lot, because this is a way I keep fit and it helps me to do my exercises daily so when my leg and foot are painful this brings some discomfort to my body and makes me feel unable to achieve the things which others take for granted.

On a good day I can do an hour of walking daily and exercise the muscles in my legs, feet and body. I do this every day, and it has helped my self-esteem a lot. I feel able and ready to tackle any tasks that I am supposed to do for the day and continue to live in the hope of a brand-new life in my body, mind, and spirit. I struggle to walk to the shops when I am in pain therefore, I ask friends and family to get me my groceries for the week until such a time when I am well enough to walk and I am healed completely by the Lord Jesus Christ. I hate suffering and if I have my own way, I don't want to have any pain of any sort in my body. I prefer being in good health and going about doing the things that I love doing. I think a lot to try and find a solution to problems, but sometimes this leads to headaches that can be severe and turn into migraines.

God humbled me in those times of pain and suffering and caused me to put my trust in him and believe that he will deliver me from the sickness I experienced. I should not think a lot on my own. I should always learn to cast my troubles to God because he cares for me and loves me so much that words cannot express. He has loved me unconditionally and therefore I have also learned the hard way to have faith and trust that God will see me through the struggles that I face. Sickness is only temporary, and I know that God's love will always surround me and will also lead me to the way of peace.

Wherever I am I have always thanked God for the gift of life and the fact that he understands my needs and will make a way for me in any time of need. I have trusted in his unfailing love and have seen him move mightily on my behalf, silencing the enemy of death upon my life and he has also given me riches in all areas of my life. I feel motivated and able to tackle whatever may come my way. God is the God who loves and restores my broken life for his glory. He is the God of yesterday, today, and forever and I am so glad to be in his fold, worshipping and serving him to the full. I pray that he will preserve my soul until eternity.

The need to be able to afford my basic needs really motivates me and causes me to act to be able to get those things which everyone is entitled to. The desire to buy myself things and afford the cost inspires me and lead me to be in the position where I can buy myself good things and help others that God brings along my path. Having been obedient to God in this way helps my self-esteem and gives pleasure that needs have been met fully. I am always drawn into the world in my life. The world of love and the world of abundance. I am always happy that I can buy myself good things and can also satisfy the needs of others that come my way and give to good causes such as a charity event.

Sometimes this may not be the case as situations at that time does not permit me to fulfil the obligations bestowed upon me. In this situation I feel that I am a failure, letting myself down and others as well but God has been good to me in those circumstances and has been telling me loudly not to worry and that things will turn around for my good soon. And eventually it does leave me with a thankful heart to God for finally answering my prayers.

I am aware of the difficulties and constraints that society placed upon me and am willing and able to see a way forward in my quest to be accepted in my environment. I therefore consider alternative ways to go about my daily task, whether alone or in a group of people.

I have considered praying as the first thing to do when faced with challenges because prayer changes things and brings about a positive result. I see that prayer works in my life and the lives of others I pray for. God is in the business of answering requests when I present them to him. He has been my source of power from which I switch on the light in prayer and draw favour and blessings from it. He is my only hope in communicating with my heavenly father. He is Lord and God alone there is no other one I know apart from him. He is all I ever needed, and he is the God who created me out of his likeness and in his image. For my life to be stable in my quest for satisfaction I must pray without ceasing and keep on holding onto the truth of the gospel. God is real and he is still a very good God to me, and I cannot live without him; he has been my shelter in those trying times of my life. God is my shield and salve.

God is my glory and the lifter up of my head. He has lifted me up from the miry day and has lifted me out of sin and shame. No longer to be held in bondage of sin and failure as he is the God who satisfies my every need. He gives me hope in my need to be accepted into the family of God. He restores my soul and leads me in pastures green for his name's sake. He does not deny himself therefore he gives me a name that I am happy to be called by – blessed, redeemed, sacrificed by the truth of the gospel. God has been with me in the Holy Spirit, and I am saved by his hand of love and mercy. Goodness is following me all throughout my days upon the earth.

I trust in his mercy and grace that one day I shall behold his glory and enter his rest forevermore. God has been patient with me because I am difficult and stubborn to deal with, but he has kept a steady hand on my life and been patiently recreating himself to me through his Word. I thank God for the day he found me and asked me to enter his presence with love that is the most fulfilling time in my whole existence. He is the God who understands me more than anyone else and he is the sacrifice for my sins and shame.

Whenever I want God to do something for me, I also think it through and determine whether I am making the right choice, then I pray about the decision I have taken in the light of that. I then wait upon him patiently for answers to my prayers – sometimes it happens straight away when he gives the correct answer and satisfies my need. Other times it takes longer for in that time he is preparing my heart for a greater blessing which will eventually blow my mind away when it is achieved.

I remember very well when I was praying fervently to come to live in London. I prayed every day about this, sometimes at prayer meetings and put my request forward. Then I started having some thoughts about this, which was to ask an uncle who was living in London to assist me while sending me a one-way ticket as I was a citizen of United Kingdom and would only need a one-way ticket to travel to London. I asked this uncle, who turned me down, then I remembered God's promises and claimed them. Another option was to go the British Embassy in Freetown seeking the ticket fare to come to London. That was a mere thought as I did not pursue that line of action, then after 4 years my brother Victor was travelling to London and promised to send me the one-way ticket I needed so that is how my prayer was answered.

Chapter 10

The setbacks I face generally

It is with great joy and endurance that I must face the battles of life head, knowing that there is always a way forward in life and everything that has happened in my life has been for a specific reason. The difficulties that have come into my life have been huge but, having said, that I tended to drift away from the care of my saviour and Lord having failed to completely put my entire trust in him and I have done things in the worldly fashion but glory to God I found my way back to God having travelled down a bumpy road for a short while.

My God has, however, been faithful and loving as I have not been in a situation in my life where I have been loved like this before. I investigated other evil sources for assistance like the new age movement and astrology, but I was going deeper and deeper into sin and the occult world of evil, but the precious hand of God held me up in those situations and caused me to think very well about where I would like to be if death struck me at that moment. It has been a strange and evil world but with God on my side all things are possible.

I tended to trust in others help rather than in God for the things I desired most in life, but all these things were not worth the effort. I would admit that in all these problems that God's hand was reaching out to me in unconditional love without me knowing it. Sometimes I found it difficult to have a good night's sleep as issues kept ringing in my mind while I lay down to sleep and I believe Satan, the devil played a part in my life at that time. I would be awake feeling sorry for myself causing me to cry out loud in the night when I was awake. The nights then seemed to be long and to go on forever as I battled with negative thoughts and tried to work out what I should do when the morning came to save me from this trap of evil that I pursued in my life. There have been lots of sacrifices made to enable me to overcome the challenges I face as I have been affected daily both day and night. I don't usually fall asleep during the day so when the terrible nights with evil came, I carried on being awake until the nights when, if I was lucky enough, I would have some sleep or otherwise it went on until the following day. But in all these uncertainties with my sleep pattern, God was showing me the way forward and caused me to put my trust in him alone and all would be perfect as he himself is a perfect God.

I had to make a few visits to the doctor to see what could be done when my sleep pattern was disturbed and discuss with family members. They told me that I possibly have strange things on my mind, and I admitted because in the night the evil forces go all out to do their work in the world, and I happen to be a victim of their traps as I had opened that door of my life for them to enter in when I slept.

I have strange dreams, not ones that someone could be proud of, as evil and Satan can follow even when one sleeps. There is a reason behind everything that happens as things do not happen by chance, whether good or bad, the results are certain to happen in a positive or negative way. Although I have been on the Lord's side for some time now, I still experience disruption in my sleep pattern. Now I know that when I am awake God wants me to meet him at the altar of prayer. To pray for myself and others together with the needs of the whole world. I do have some rest in the night now although I am usually up at between 4-5 am in the morning most days as I have an appointment with my God to meet him at the altar of prayer. These sessions of prayer have been so rewarding and positive as the whole day folds around and things gets on very well indeed and I appear to have a more positive outlook on life now than before. You are all included in my prayers daily and I thank God for this sustaining grace to enable me to keep the appointment with him. I would not do this alone except God be with me therefore I do give thanks to almighty God for making all this possible. I know now that when the evil spirits roaming around seeking their victims. I am up in the night counteracting their performance through the prayers. I am offering for myself and for everyone in the world. And great and mighty things have been accomplished in heaven + that is affecting us all here on earth. During these sessions of dry seasons due to the wickedness I always find myself in the presence of God as God leads and as the spirit of God prompts me to do so. I am no longer fearful of the unknown mission, but I count everyday as a blessing from God if I continue to live upon the earth. Things are going smoothly for me now taking one day as it comes and committing everything to God in prayer and waiting upon him to have his way in my life and others I pray for.

I want to be under God's rule which I think is the best way forward according to the Bible which is God's word delivered to mankind therefore as a friend of Jesus Christ who paid the debt of love for my sins on the cross where he died and rose again on the third day and ascended into heaven where he is at the right hand of God praying and interceding for me. I have forsaken all worldly pleasures and made up my mind to follow him and him alone and crown him Lord of my life. He is my master and Lord, and I am in an intimate relationship with the father and the son now. He did not provide me an easy life but says that he will be there with me along the way. God moved on my behalf through all the scenes of life as they keep on changing. In fact, God doesn't want me to have Satan anymore. He is a jealous God, all of him or none of him. He does not share his glory with Satan and since I trusted him fully many years ago I have endeavoured to put my total confidence and trust in God alone and not yield to my own abilities or knowledge of what I believe he is but to feed my spirit on the Bible which is God's word and God has been my protector and guide ever since I decided to follow him and put him in first place in my life. The challenges of life are sometimes great to bear but God's love always surrounds me and brings me through.

The dark ages did not get me anywhere, I was spending more money on consultations and not getting the result I was hoping for, but thanks be to God for his abundant mercy and love, which lifted me out of the pit of hell and rescued me from the hand of the deceiver and destroyer of my soul. Now I am certain that God almighty is the only true God who needs to be worshipped and adored. Nothing in my life can ever be able to separate me from his unconditional love. He has loved me even though I stray from his hand like a lost sheep. He speaks to me through the Bible. I know what I have to do to live a successful life. Nothing is hidden from him. He knows all things and has been my creator, forming me in his image and out of his likeness and telling me to replenish the earth and subdue it. It is the ever-loving God the creator of the universe. I thank God I am part of his kingdom here on earth.

While I was growing up as a little girl my sexual life was being abused by my uncle. This is my mum's sister's husband in Sierra Leone as at that time I was living there, and he too was living in the family house together with my aunt his wife and other members of my family. I spent years being sexually abused at the hands of this notorious uncle who thought much about himself. And because he had money and everyone in the family respected him so much as not to think that he could have had sex with me at the time. He used to threaten me not to say a word to my parents about the incident and I kept quiet. Now I am sharing and voicing my pain in this matter. Things were very difficult for us living in Sierra Leone, so much poverty and lack and one could not figure where the next meal was going to come from daily. He had the money and the power within his reach and took advantage of me then. I was afraid of him so much that I kept it a secret from everyone else within the family. His name is Victor Johnson and he is currently living in America.

Moving over to London to live and settle down in life I was also the victim of sexual abuse from another uncle, in this instance my dad's cousin when I was trying to find my way around London in 1988. I contacted him for help to write a reference for me to enter university at Kingston to study for a course in Social Science. He then used his position to sexually abuse me as well. So, in my life I have had two known well-respected family members who misused their trust and took matters into their own hands to devour what God created in me. I felt hurt and troubled in mind and body, soul and spirit at this horrible event in life that I had to endure.

There are very wicked and cruel people who take the chance to distort what God has established in his word. I have come through these horrible experiences in sexual abuse from these two family members as God has finally healed me from the hurt and pain suffered because of these evil acts by these two people whom I highly respected in my life. I have forgiven them truly because I want to move forward with my life and to tap into all that God has in store for me as the future seems bright and prosperous. I am grateful to God that deliverance occurred in my life, and I am free from these abuses I suffered.

The other uncle still lives here in London and is called Chandu Magsking but God has kept me away from him so much so that I don't keep in touch with him anymore. Life is full of strange happenings in my quest to put my foot firmly on the ground, but I am grateful for God for his healing hand upon my life and the difference the blood of Jesus makes in my life as I continue to trust and serve him with my whole heart. There are lots of evil people about, one cannot trust people these days as evil sweeps through our world at such a great pace.

However, God is still on the throne and will rescue me from all evil people like these two family members who misused their trust and confidence with me. I had to struggle a lot with these emotions as I felt let down by members of my immediate family I trusted. I had to turn to God in prayer for restoration and healing I so desperately needed at these times of my life.

God is gracious and loving and I could hear him speak to me through the word of God (the Bible) that in the world you will have troubles but be of good cheer I have overcome the world. I have trusted and believed that God in his goodness will save me from being abused further in this way or by any other way that Satan tends to come into my life. Satan is a defeated force and father of kings, but God's grace and mercy and love saved me through and through and today I can say that hitherto hath the Lord helped me overcome these sources of abuse and unwanted contacts from my abusers.

Nothing is impossible with God, and he makes everything beautiful in his time. No matter what I have been through in life God's love still leads me on and takes me from one glory to another with the Holy Spirit being my helper. I do realise the fact that I am living in a troubled world and there are bad people about but God in his love will deliver me from such people and I just must put my trust and confidence in God alone.

I experienced lots of fear and intimidation because of the abuse I suffered and could only hope and pray that things would sort themselves out and therefore enable me to live a God-fearing life. I feel such sadness that I had to endure such cruelty at the hands of people I trusted and respected, having done all I could to escape from turmoil and suffering. I felt badly let down and distraught and found it difficult to trust men again. But over the years God has healed me from the pain and the disappointment I endured. When things like this happen in your family circle you have reason to fear and feel abandoned.

However, when all hope is lost, I can cling on to God almighty for deliverance and help when I need him most. He is nearer to me than when I first believed. Nothing in his sight goes unnoticed. He is all powerful and someone I can put my trust and confidence in. The true God who is the creator of the universe is my guide and helper. He has bought me back with his son Jesus Christ through the death, burial and resurrection of a saviour and I am grateful for this. He is the reason I am living now and I am confident that he will see me through the various challenges I face in my life. Nothing is impossible with God he sees my pain and troubles and is always with me

Once there is life, there is hope. I thank God that although I felt suicidal yet his loving care surrounds and strengthens me to move on in life and forget the past and abusive things and the sinful habits I engaged in.

Luckily for me, I found my way in life through the prompting of the Holy Spirit who is at work in my life. God has not forgotten me, he is there beside me through all the troubles of life. I try to read my Bible every day and pray as well so that I can express myself to God and let him know how I am feeling and then investigate the Bible for comfort and just be still in his presence and allow him to speak to me and give me encouragement. During those dark days I could not figure anything out. I was totally lost in the darkness of my world but God's helping hand reaching out to me has made me realise how much he loves me. I will never forget where God has brought me from when I could not speak to anyone about my troubles yet could speak to him in prayer and he revealed himself to me through his word, the Bible. God in his love and grace promised to restore all the lost years I spent in vanity toiling over ill behaviour from people I trusted and highly respected and he took me by the arm and guided me along the way.

He is faithful and keeps his promises and is ever present in my day-to-day chores. He is the one and only one in whom I can trust. All others are sinful humans and have caused me to doubt their integrity. I have come a long way in my journey of life but since I believed that God in his love is all I ever wanted, he has been sustaining and meeting my every need. I don't know what would have become of me if I had not got God on my side to help me out in my troubles and pain. I probably would have been dead by now and gone to hell, but thanks be to God who is the ultimate gift to mankind

Humans cannot do without a loving God who means the best for his children. He is sufficient for me, I can say with confidence and power that God is a good God not willing to let me perish but to come to a personal relationship with him and live a life of peace, harmony, and freedom in Christ. God gave me something when I had nothing to offer except my whole life in readiness for his power to operate in my life. I will ever be grateful to God for coming through for me and helping me to get through these troubles I suffered from the hands of people I trusted. I can now say that I know God fully and truly and can confidently say that Jesus is my saviour and Lord, and I can rely on his word to sustain me.

I had been in a dark place in my life due to the death of my father and the abuse I suffered from family members and various other challenges. I face these in my Christian walk with God but in all the things that transpired I am able and ready to hold onto the faith and pursue my God given talents and abilities and continue to carry on trusting and believing God will make a way for me as I seek to do his will and to become obedient to his commandments.

God has shone his light brightly in my path and now I can clearly see my way forward. The difficulties will still be there but one thing I know is that God will carry me through it all and deliver me from the hand of the oppressor.

There is no turning back for me, it is all of me and I am determined to do all in my power to please God and serve him fully in whatsoever capacity he chooses me to do so. At least the fear does not bother me anymore as God gives me hope and trust to present myself in a positive manner before him daily in prayer and the reading of God's word. Now these days I don't care anymore about the injustice suffered if God is my helper, he is enough for me. He is the one now in control of my life. I have lived a long time now on my own terms. Now I opened the door to God to pilot me through life's journey because if I want to do it by myself, I may fail and get into trouble again with wicked people so now it's all about Jesus and he is the only true Messiah and saviour in my life.

I trust him and confidently say that I am now what I am due to his intervention. Nothing can be simpler than this. My whole life has been a series of trouble here and there trying to find my grip in life as the devourer has had the better of me and thinks he can own me fully when I belong to Jesus. He suffered and died and paid the debt I could not pay. I am totally sold to God and Jesus is my only sacrificial lamb that was slain for my sins. I have been rescued by his mighty hand and nothing can by any means hurt me anymore. He has healed my wounds and sees me overcome the obstacles which Satan and his angels put in my path. I thank my God upon every reminder he has done for me because without him I am nothing. He never leaves me, nor has he forsaken me. He is always with me wherever I go.

I am very careful and cautious now with people because of the hurt and pain I suffered in the past, but having said that I have to study an individual properly to put me on the right path of a relationship with anyone before opening up to them. I know this may seem mean, but I have no choice other than to protect myself fully and take extra care with my dealing with people especially family members.

Having said that I had a family member – my cousin – who telephoned me and wanted me to visit him in London. When I went over and we were chatting I realised that the reason he wanted me to visit him was for him to have sexual intercourse with me. I didn't yield to that demand. I quickly went out of his house and came home. Luckily, God was with me at the time and last year he died. Heaven knows where that soul must have got to. I don't know but do I seem to be attracted to the opposite sex, especially family members? I don't know. I do believe that Satan is stirring up all these troubles for me and setting a trap for me to enter, but thanks be to God for the victory to overcome the demands of the evil one.

It was a very surprising demand and daring action on his part to have even taken the pains to tell me to come over for such an evil act. I don't believe how people can act in such a brutal way to further satisfy their sexual urges. I want to be grateful to God for making a way for me to be able to escape from it all. Heaven only knows what kind of a sad individual he was and how he could even think about making such gestures to me.

I concluded that I am not safe even within my own family members and I had to run away to a far place to get away from all these sexual demands. Even uphill now, I feel fearful to approach anyone of my male family members in fear that a worse action may occur in the future. But another voice tells me not to be fearful of human beings but to wait, trusting God for protection and care and his love will carry me through the rest of the days I have here on planet earth. God is with me through the troubles I face, and he will carry me onto the next level of development in my walk of faith. Knowing for sure that he is able to do even more for me than I dare to think or imagine. I am assured that the pain and suffering of yesterday has gone, and today is a bright new day and there is a future in which God controls my life.

No attack of the devil will triumph over me because God shields me with his love and protection. Had I not known him yet as my God in him whom I trust I would have gone mental, or be dead by now, but all praise and thanks to God who gives me the victory in Jesus Christ my Lord. I am fascinated by the word of God in the Bible, that Jesus is praying for me, interceding to the father on my behalf and he has blessed me with his spirit who is living in my heart. All the distrust and negative behaviour I suffered God has used it to bring out the best in my life and used my experience to help others in similar situations in life. I use my experience to help others who have been bound by the acts of the evil done and reader whatsoever emotional support that is needed at that time in history. I also share my testimony with who believe and thereby encourage them to continue to put their trust in God for deliverance and to provide for their every need. Things are not good now but one thing I know is that God is always with me in my struggles and sees through me through gently. One day at a time. It is not all rosy, but I am getting there gradually with the help of God and the few people I am in contact with. Thankfully there are some good ones about these days as well.

My experience has strengthened me, and I am now able to face head-on any troubles that await me in the future because I know and trust that God on his throne in heaven will deliver and help me achieve my God given talents and make me into a new and refined individual serving my local community in the best possible way.

When I hear of bad things happening to good people, I tend to think God 'Where you in all this? Show up in their situation and put the devil to shame and deliver your people from the hands of the oppressor whose duty it is to destroy us totally and causes us to flee from the control of God.' But God be thanks that he is the ultimate God above every other God on earth and when we choose to trust him and accept his love into our hearts, he makes all things beautiful in his time.

I am involved in my local church here in Wimbledon. I also belong to a Bible study group where we support and pray for each other's needs. I find these groups of worship very helpful as God is leading and directing every affair of my life because I can speak in confidence with others in my group and they in turn encourage and pray for me as well. No man is an island, we rely on each other, and God is making it possible for me to share my experience with the group and great and mighty things have been accomplished there with people in my group.

I came to realise that not everyone that smiles at me is my friend. Friends on the other hand I can suggest are those who are there for me at the rough times and as well as at the good times. They don't judge me but support me in what I am going through now so many tears have been shed over night that causes me to ponder whether it is worth it. I don't have that many friends but I have a few that I can count on if needs be. They are my inner circle although we don't meet up regularly as we are supposed to do due to the fact that we are all in different areas of the world and doing our own thing but we tend to make phone contact often and hear of what the good Lord is doing in each of our lives.

I thank God for the few friends I have as they have been there for me through the dark times and the good times. I do appreciate them in my life and pray for them regularly that God continues to keep us all in his love and care. There is no better way to express my gratitude for my friends for the way they have stood alongside me in all the troubles and joy that life brings in my life. I am praying that the love continues to bond within us into others and the radiance of his divine nature will be seen in all that we do to the glory of God. May God bless them so much for caring for me in this way.

I have 4 siblings including one half-brother who lives in Sierra Leone. My older sister Daphne went to live with our grandmother, my dad's mum, until she passed away and I and my brother and sister lived with our parents in Sierra Leone for the best part of our lives until we travelled to London to settle down. During our stay back in Freetown we did not have much as is the norm for people living in third world countries and Sierra Leone is the poorest country in the world. There was not much in terms of abilities to succeed at a great level. Things were very difficult and hard. I remember as a young girl growing up that even food to eat was a problem. We did not have the meals for the family to survive. We were barely surviving on hand outs and not much hope to live, for we were poverty stricken. Things were so bad that we sometimes had to sleep on an empty stomach. Nothing to look for, all hopes dashed. This is when my uncle abused his position because he had money and was providing for his family very well. My mother Mrs Lois Saire favours Victor my brother more than any of us. Victor could do nothing wrong in her eyes that was worth discipline. She loved him so much to defend him whenever he did something wrong to myself and my sister.

I found this injustice hard to bear as we were punished severely for what Victor did to us that made us retaliate and beat him. In those days beating was acceptable, and my mum used to beat the hell out of me for any wrongdoing to Victor our brother. There was nothing I could do about it so I was made to suffer in silence. I had a mother who did not love me, and I find it hard to bear because I was looking for acceptance in my mother to no avail. Everything looked like a dead-end road for me.

I was only appreciated and loved by my dad although he had troubles providing for the family and my needs. I was looking to God for comfort at those times in which I was unfairly treated by my mother and was privileged to be attending a church called Bethel Temple and got involved with the youth groups there and interacted well with other youths about my age. I came to realise that if mother's love was not forthcoming let me try another avenue to see if my acceptance of love will be welcome. Then I was introduced to the Holy Spirit by the Lord and came into a love match relationship with God and the saviour Jesus Christ who sacrificed his life for me to be part of his kingdom here on earth. I thank God I took the chance to have a personal relationship with Jesus.

I was involved in all aspects of the worship in my local church and took an active part in ministry in the hospital with a group of my fellow worshippers where after the Sunday service in church we went to the Connaught hospital to hold a service and pray for the sick. I took a lot of interest in this sort of ministry as God led me to do so and had a strong desire to minister to the sick in this way and was also in the position to see lots of miracles happen in people's lives. People who were miraculously healed from all manner of diseases and sicknesses. We took the chance sometimes to lay hands on the sick and pronounced them healed in the name of Jesus and that's what happened in our ministry. It was very exciting to be able to deliver the gospel message of salvation as well to the sick as they lay in bed waiting for God to intervene in their situation. In all these things I was able to witness the lame walking and throwing away their crutches. The blind seeing and lots of other miracles happened during our sessions of ministry to God's people. It brought so much joy in my heart to see God manifesting his power through us as we sought to be obedient to his will and minister to the people of God.

The youth group I belonged to was very closely knit and we always looked forward to what God was going to do next in our encounter with his work for the sick and suffering that we ministered to.

God was using me in that capacity to deliver the word of salvation to the people of God. God manifested his power through us as many people who witnessed the acts of God in our midst gave their lives to Christ and decided to follow him fully from then. I do believe that in my present situation God is still fulfilling his plans in my life and is still using me to bring hope, restoration and deliverance to his people. I always feel that I do have the gift of healing and whenever I call upon him for the healing of people in my care, I see him bring hope and restoration for their health to them.

I am deeply honoured and appreciate God for using me in this way to develop his kingdom here on earth. I desire the gift and I believe that God has blessed me within because all he requires of me is to ask him for whatsoever, I want, and he will give it to me. He has blessed me these days with such blessings in the heavenly realm that my mouth is too small to give him thanks for all his tender mercies and love he has bestowed upon me. Despite the troubles I have been through God has said to me that he has not finished with me yet, there is a bright future ahead of me and I will see the goodness of God in the hand of the living if I keep my own part of the bargain and walk in obedience to his will.

With God by my side, I believe that all things are within my reach, and I just must possess my possession in his kingdom. Every time I pray, I present my case to him and ask that he use me to his glory to build his kingdom here on earth and I am grateful to the people he brings along my path to enable me to fulfil my God given talent and be a good citizen here on earth that affects the call to heaven someday as God is my keeper.

I have faith that is enough to move the obstacles in my life and that of others and I have been called by God to pray for as I do delight in interceding for other people's needs as well. In the light of my calling, I have been able to see God answer my prayers for my own needs and that of the needs of others I pray for. God is a good God, not willing that any should perish but that we all in the whole world will come to true repentance of faith and serve our local communities. He wants to use us for his glory to make the unbelievers know that yes indeed there is a true God who deserves our praise and worship. God is working his purpose out in my life. I have always felt warm and accepted by God for his divine interaction and sustaining grace bestowed upon me and

I have manifested his plans in every area of my life as I seek to walk in his ways and do my bidding.

I am a go-getter kind of person. If I want something I persevere until I finally get it. I don't give in easily to negative demands because I believe that if I pray for anything I need, God will answer and supply that need in my life in his own time and for his glory because I will end up thanking him again for his provision so that the glory goes to him.

There is a good reason why God does not answer me immediately when I make any requests to him in prayer. H sometimes wants me to wait until the fullness of time because he can give me what I have asked for so in the light of this I persistently continue in prayer waiting for the manifestation of his will in my life.

There are times in my life when I feel very desperate in need of something and do want an immediate answer when I pray for it, like coming to live in the UK after much hardship in Sierra Leone but God kept me waiting for some time before we could finally make it possible for me to travel to London to live because I was originally born here in London Hammersmith and also I was going to come back home to make a future that God has given me for me and my family. I then realised after coming to London that things were not too favourable in London either. There was vast racism here to its highest degree and had I come to live when I wanted to, I might have become so saddened to be in the position where I would be facing racism from all angles of the society because the white people were ignorant about us black people living in the UK.

Nowadays it is much better although there is to some degree of racism going on behind closed doors but not openly.

I do accept everybody God brings my way. I may feel different from them, but I am not in the position to judge a man when God so loved them to send his only son to die for their sins as well so if God loved us all in the world, we ought also to love everybody else that comes along our path. I do not discriminate ever, I never will because ignorance of the laws of God is no excuse to display such negative notions and forms imagery about one's status in life.

There has always been perfect timing for me with my God. I understand the way God works in my life because he is the guiding hand of all I need in life. Sometimes it's hard to wait as the situation I find myself in is desperate but with a little more patience with thanksgiving things unfold themselves as the days go by. God is no respecter of a person and does not wait on any man, but I can now say that my confidence is in him alone.

I have made some investments that have gone bust. Aspire investment and Mirror Trading investment to name just a couple and all monies I invested in these companies have gone. No one was ever able to account for the losses I suffered. No not one. I was left high and dry in the wilderness of sin with no one to account for my money. I had invested quite a lot of money in these companies, thinking that my investments would grow over time and therefore cause me to reap the benefit of my labour. I worked hard for my money so to see my money going down the drain like this was heart breaking and sad. There was no one to explain to me about the whereabouts of my money. Not a soul. But I take it to be that Satan had his hands on it and has done it to suit his needs. There are lots of evil people around preying on innocent people like me to get the better of them. But God on his throne is watching us all the time and, in his goodness, will bring justice. I do pray for these so-called criminals to be made accountable for their actions and I know that one day things will be done to bring me to an expected end of these tests. I don't sit around I always work, day and night to make a living.

In fact, the gentleman who introduced the Mirror Trading investment to me approached me again about another investment plan which he thinks is more secure and profitable, but I turned the idea down because I have been left bruised with this one and was fearful of another repeat of the process to happen to me. Once attracted, left bruised and dry was my visitor in this area of getting some money working for me. I can recall his conversation to me via email telling me how successful I will become if I just put this situation behind me which is painful and move forward with my life, but I do not want to take any more chances. Instead, I prefer to invest in the kingdom of God, supporting Christian work where my proceeds will yield rewards for me over time here on earth and store some treasures in heaven for eternity. I think this is the best way forward for me as I seek to deliver God's standard of living for myself, the world around me and those disadvantaged lives whom God will draw to me to assist financially.

I do pray every day that the brains behind the investment will see some sense in their actions and become accountable to me for the loss of my money and have the decency to pay back with interest all that I am legally owed, and I trust in God that one day things will be sorted out so that finally we can all live in peace and move on with our separate lives.

However long it takes I am prepared to press on for concrete solutions to the whole matter to enable me to be more cautious and for it to not repeat itself ever again. I am so hurt that I tend to keep it a secret from family members especially because they don't need to know what pains and lack I suffered from these unscrupulous people who only think of themselves.

Now I feel trapped but hoping that freedom will locate me as I seek to continue in prayer to my God who watches over me to fulfil his plan and purpose for my life. Satan is everywhere waging war with me in my quest to be settled in my emotions. I can recall times I have cried and think that God is far away from me when these unhappy moments strike me, but he is nearer than when I believe and reaches his hand of love towards me all the time. Things are going to get better since he is in my boat and is calming the storms of life that I face.

There are lots of evil people about these days and one has to be careful of who one interacts with as these wicked and evil people are so clever in their actions and use their skills of deceit to con us.

Chapter 11

The Reality of My Life

Notwithstanding that there are issues in my life that I must deal with personally and sometimes can pose a threat to my real existence on this earth. I sometimes wonder where I can gain strength to fight the difficulties and troubles I face. I am left with the need to be thrown into God's loving arms. If I try alone things become much more difficult so I try as hard as I can to let go and allow God to have his way, but there are times in my life when I feel inadequate, almost quitting the journey of faith and trusting in my own understanding.

This is not enough to see me through the challenges I face daily but throwing all to Jesus' feet gives me that upper hand to know that I am not alone, and God is in the journey with me, holding my hands in his and leading me into victory. The path I walk in is dark but there is always light at the end of the tunnel as Jesus is leading the way to victory. I then realise his loving arms outstretched to save and deliver me from evil and establish my feet on that firm foundation. I put my trust in people who used and abused me, and some do betray my trust in them. Where can I go for help? Only to the Lord who rules the universe. He is my only hope and joy, and he satisfied my longing to be integrated into the society in which I live now. It is not by accident that I live here in London, it is all by God's divine plan and purpose for my life that I live and surrender to his will generally. Because nothing is too difficult for God, he is my provider, and he sustains me and helps me get back on track to discover my true self-image for living in a broken world. My faith is growing stronger and stronger every day and I can see God's hand in everything I do for his glory. He comes alongside me and helps me get to winning ways as my situation is dark and dreary but faith in the Lord Jesus and willingness to obey his voice keeps me on the right path to victory.

I am usually go to bed early in the night therefore miss the midnight prayers but wake up early in the morning round about 4am to offer my prayers to God and commit the day into his hand. Whenever I do, I feel the day goes on well and I am able to achieve lots of things that I am supposed to do for a day done well.

I have some friends who I disappoint for being unable to get on Zoom in the early evenings time simply because I am usually asleep at that time. I have explained my situation to them and trust that they can understand if I am unable to log in on the Bible study Zoom meetings on a Wednesday evening when it is being held. I feel guilty sometimes for letting the folks down by my absence, but this is how things are with me. Early to bed early to rise and the important part of it is that I do say my prayers at 4am in the morning first thing when I wake up and prayer for everything and everyone that God lays on my heart.

I have developed the habit to pray first thing in the morning before I do anything else in the house and in between chores say some more prayers as the day goes on and I have found it helpful. Because if you are in a relationship with someone you want to always speak to them first thing when you wake up. So, it is with my God I have cultivated a plan to whisper a prayer regularly at home.

Another project I have taken up is the act of fasting. Since October 2019 the Lord has impressed it on my mind to observe the fast regularly, so the last 3 days of the month I observe a fast where my soul reaches out to God and my body becomes weak in the process of calling upon God for my daily needs and that of others as well as he has called me to intercede for the peoples of the earth, so whenever I have a prayer request I also pray and fast and present all our needs to God in prayer.

During lockdown I find myself reading more of the Bible and this has enabled me to hear what God is saying to me about the issues of life that I am treading on. Life is not easy, Jesus himself did not have an easy road therefore as a follower of Jesus I should be prepared to face trials and tribulations but since I rely on God's power to sore and rescue me from danger, he will certainly come through for me and give me victory along the way. I have come a long way to be in the position to hear from God and just relax and let him carry me through life's journey with no struggles at all on my part. I don't have to relish him at all as he is all knowing and will perfect that which concerns me. I have a thorn in the flesh, now my leg is very painful and keeps me awake at night especially. I have tried painkillers, but the pain has still not left my leg. I am just trusting and praying to God that hopefully I will be delivered from this pain that is making life a bit uneasy for me at this present time.

All things are in God's hands and according to his will he will heal and deliver me from this pain that the doctors said is a strained ligament and will take 8 weeks to go away. Still trusting and believing that a miracle will happen sooner than when I first believed. I am still hanging on for my breakthrough which will come soon, and I can celebrate in style with worship and dancing to the Lord my God for his healing hand upon my life and for giving me a mighty good sleep.

I can still walk but it's painful when I take steps even if it is a little bit at a time. The pain is in the leg part of my ligament. I know God will deliver me but how soon I don't know. I just keep on praying that I get through the day carefully with no issues to deal with.

I must do small chores and sit down for a while before doing another one as the pain is severe. I fell in the middle of the road when the snow was still on the ground after a few days. As a result, I injured my ligament and since then I have been in pain and so severely that I find walking a bit of a problem now. Only God can heal and set me free from pain.

The devil meant evil for me, but God will turn my situation around for his glory. So that the praise will finally go to him I am just trusting and believing in God that I am set free from suffering. I claim the blood of Jesus on my leg and command the devil to let go and let God have his way in my life. I am totally sold to the will of God and Satan has no part with me as I am a child of God and believe that no weapon fashioned against me shall prosper but everything will be manifested for God's glory.

I do believe that the days of miracles are not yet over, only faith in the Lord Jesus Christ and his power to save will deliver me from this evil which has befallen me.

Nothing is impossible with God because if he has already done it for me before, he surely will do it again for me now. I trust in him to deliver and rescue me from the arms of the devil.

Before I used to have migraines, very severe headaches. I then discovered that it is because I was perming my hair for such a long time. So, I stopped perming my hair but now put it in plaits and try to grow it naturally. Since I stopped perming the headaches have stopped. Thanks be to God all I needed was a bit of adjustment to my everyday appearance. Thanks be to God I don't have headaches anymore, totally healed by the power of God. This is something that I practised doing so that I can be free from the frequent headaches that I experienced.

I am passionate about the environment and the contribution I could make in it to keep it clean and healthy. Therefore, I have pursued cleaning rules in and around my home and cut the grass often so that it looks good. I usually do it with another resident who also takes pleasure in gardening and keeping the area looking clean and tidy.

I like to spend my moments listening to Radio Premier Christian radio station which I find very inspiring especially during the lockdown when I spent much of the time at home. It helps me to focus more on God and my position in the universe and my contribution to the society in which I belong. Premier Christian radio station has been a lifeline for me, and a godsend to my spiritual needs. I find that I grow daily listening to presenters delivering the gospel of truth to the nation and around the globe. I also participate in activities delivered by the radio station, like when there are prayers offered, I join in and pray as well. I feel drawn towards the hope that is within me because I can make a difference spiritually to the world I live in and establish a common purpose for living. I would therefore like to take this chance to recommend Premier Christian station to others who are searching for answers to their questions as many needs are met through general prayers offered on air and lots of healings also takes place by just tuning in and listening to the presenters as they deliver the word of truth to the dying world.

I don't know where I would be today because it helps me a lot in my Christian journey of faith, and I am fully grateful to God for the opportunity to partake in the gospel of Christ through various speakers from various cultures and backgrounds but with one common purpose, which is to make Christ known and to be a living embodiment of his love and grace.

I make regular donations to Premier because I feel led by God to support the listeners station as it also blesses me spiritually and enables me to live a God fearing life and one way to show my appreciation to God for his blessings is to give back a little money of what he has blessed me with to Premier so that the station can continue its work to broadcast to the nation because it's a listening supportive programme and receives no funding from the UK government at all. So, my contribution will go a long way to reach the lost and dying so that more people will hear about the saving grace of our Lord Jesus Christ and be helped by it. I love all the programmes on the radio I usually tune into the station just after my morning devotion and keep it on all day until bedtime.

I started listening to the radio station 25 years ago when a friend from church told me about it and says that it will help me in my Christian journey. So, I immediately searched for the station on the radio 1305 AM, on the TV 725 Freeview and since then I have been hooked on it. It never leaves my sight whenever I am home it is always on. It's a source of great strength and power to my journey of life and has enabled me to be the person I am today due to the help of God and applying the teaching to my everyday life. It has also helped to shape my prayer life a whole lot more these latter days of my life during the lockdown. I am humbled and honoured to be a part of what God is doing in my life at this present time. Nothing has been left to chance as I have been able to seize every opportunity and make the most out of a positive life. My sorrow and troubles are a thing of the past because I know that the presence of God is with me at all times in the house even though I am alone, yet I don't feel lonely as the Lord himself is beside me always. The radio station is my daily companion. I rely on it for daily spiritual food and blessings, therefore I am committed to act in a positive manner towards the calling of God upon my life.

I have been a frequent worshipper at the Emmanuel church Wimbledon where I meet with other worshippers to worship God in the beauty of his holiness and have been privileged to participate in other activities of the church life. I belong to the Tuesday Bible study group where we now meet on Zoom to study the Bible with other Christian folks, all ladies. I then took part in Sunday school activities for the 2-year-olds in church and also belong to the persecuted church prayer meeting that meets every second Sunday afternoon in church to pray for our brothers and sisters who are being persecuted for their faith all over the world.

I have been active in Christian service, and I take great pleasure in serving the Lord and others in my church family. It is easily accessible for me since I live only 15 minutes' walk from the church and can attend on time and regularly as the Lord permits me to do. I tried my level best to let no situations that are contrary to my beliefs get in the way of my faith and weigh up every idea that comes to mind thoroughly before taking the appropriate action. One thing I do not want is to live in regret for taking the wrong actions. So, I do pray a lot about issues and think through it sensibly before concluding.

I can make friends at church. During the prayer sessions after the Bible study meetings, I can share needs and share those burdens that I am faced with now and other members of the group pray for such requests. This is a fascinating thing and makes me be assured that others have my back covered as well in prayers. When there is a testimony, I must share with the group I usually bring it along to the attention of members and offer thanks unto God for what he has done. The members that I worshipped with are open-minded and welcome me at any time to discuss issues of interest and prayers for God to move in those situations. This has been tremendous help to my Christian journey of faith as life is usually tough going but knowing that other people do care gives me that peace of mind. There is no better way than when two people agree in prayer over one thing and God always promises to meet us at the point of our needs and those requests offered in prayer have certainly been answered. God is good, God who delights in the affairs of his children. Before lockdown I was always looking forward to church meetings to worship and then afterwards have a chat over coffee with members of the church. The people I worship with are friendly and welcome me with open arms.

Sometime ago I was in debt for mis-management of my money and rent was accrued and my landlord was threatening me with eviction. My brother Victor put me in touch with an organisation called Christians Against Poverty who took my case onboard. They contacted the church to pay the amount I owed which was £5,000. The church willingly paid the amount, and I was then able to continue living in my current flat and have since been able to pay the rent when due. I owe a lot to the church and its members and pray that this gesture of goodwill will continue until eternity. One may not know what the future holds but one thing for certain is that God oversees everything about our lives, so with that in mind I try to live a life that is pleasing and acceptable to God. When I need a large purchase and don't have the money to buy it immediately there is a couple in church I approach who agree to loan me money without interest. I find this very helpful because if I was to borrow from other financial institutions, they would require interest on top of the amount I borrow but this couple don't charge me any interest. What I borrow is what I pay back and nothing more added on top. So, I thank God that he is my provider and sees me through financially.

Recently Jenner my son needed £1,000 to repair his bike. I approached Jan and Steve at church. This is the couple who loan me money when I am in need, and they were very willing to lend me the money and told me that I should let Jenner pay it all back himself which he agreed to do. This is very good of them, and it helps me to know that if I can't afford something now I can rely on them for financial assistance. I already borrowed money from Jan and Steve 3 years ago to decorate my flat and they loaned me £3,000 to get everything done. I thank God that I belong to a church where I can get help from whenever I need. It's an ongoing process because Jesus teaches us to show brotherly/sisterly love and kindness to each other. This is the fulfilment of God's commands.

During this pandemic, with lockdown taking a toll on our individual lives and churches closed because of this, only live streaming was allowed. I find myself worshipping at home with premier and Tuesdays on Zoom with my Bible study group. Still missing seeing each other as we used to and interacting and having chats and a cup of tea during sessions. With the vaccination given now things are beginning to ease down slowly and not too long now we shall be able to meet again for fellowship with each other.

My mother is very supportive of me attending Emmanuel church because she said to me that if the church is helping me financially when I get into trouble with my rent it is worth staying there and continuing to serve God there as well as others in my care. I think she is right in saying that to me and I will continue to worship and be a part of what is going on over here in Wimbledon and making a difference in the society to which I belong.

I am settled here in church because I have made a lot of friends and continue to seek other ways of service for the Kingdom's sake. I do visit other churches but not for too long especially my friends' church when they have special occasions, and I am invited to attend. I had to support my friends church on those rare occasions and worship there sometimes but will stick with Emmanuel church come what may.

I was brought up a Pentecostal but find myself now giving and worshipping at an evangelical Church of England church here in Wimbledon, a journey I treasured so much as s it is, as the Bible teaches, second to none. I do enjoy every bit of it and always apply myself fully to the worship although Satan knowing what he's like tries to take my attention from the worship. But the focus is the most important factor for me. I try to concentrate on the worship to avoid all distractions and commune with my God. This is vital to my spiritual uplifting and creates a vacuum of praise and adoration to the God we serve. There are no perfect settings in church life as everyone has got their own flaws that they carry with them into the presence of God. This is where concession is made into righteousness, and we then discover our role in the society in which we belong. I just want to live free from the troubles that surround us in this world and be a good citizen in my country, but the pressure of life is kicking against me and the devil is trying in all his power to keep me away from God who created me in his likeness and placed me on this earth to fulfil his purpose for living.

It is not an easy road for me but with the help of God my master and friend I am winning against all odds to be integrated into the wider society. Certainly, nothing is impossible with God. He fills my life with his spirit who leads me into everlasting life. There are various storms on my pathway, but I thank God that I take one step along the way with God by my side to brighten the journey and he has been faithful in seeing me through the various trials that I face.

My health is my problem now which I am battling, but I am depending upon God for victory and deliverance in this matter. I find that I can't sleep well at night because of it as I am in so much pain I wake up in the middle of the night but I have an anchor that catches the solid route of Christ. I am hanging in there for my breakthrough. I have been supported by family members and friends in this situation. They have been a shoulder to cry on at these painful moments currently in my life.

I strained my ligament a while ago and since then I have had a painful leg which causes walking to be very difficult for me now. But I trust God to carry this load away from me soon. The doctor says that it takes 8 weeks for the pain to cease but I am still suffering and believing in God for a miracle in this respect. The doctor's verdict is not final. I have a miracle working God and call upon him in times of my pain and suffering to intercede and bring me to victory. I rely on the promises of Jesus in that he tells me that he will never leave me nor forsake me so when troubles come my way I go into prayer and pour my heart out to almighty God and ask him to help me overcome my troubles and set me free from pain.

I also suffer from high blood pressure but it's being controlled by medication. It's been some time now since I had to see the doctor about it, and I thank God that everything is going on nicely now on that front. I do take medication for it every day and according to doctor's orders drink 1.5 litres of water daily and make the effort to eat fruits. There has however been an adjustment to my healthy eating as I do eat sensibly and try not to put the weight on as this has been a problem for me in the past. I eat twice a day. Lunch and dinner and drink lots of water all through the day. In fact, when things get tough, and I am about to give up I say a last pray to God and invite him to take full control of the situation and rescue me from the furnace I am in at that time, and he has always come through for me at the dying moment to deliver me from the hand of the devourer. God is all I have now I can't live without him by my side. The first thing I do in the morning when I wake up, after I have made myself a cup of tea, is to pray and commit the day into his hand. Doing this regularly makes the day go on smoothly with no problems and I am assured of his guidance and care.

Sometimes Satan tries to keep me away from God and he brings all sorts of negative things to my mind, but I am certain that God is always true to his word and will perfect his will and purpose in my life. I am faced with trials on every corner but one thing for sure is that God is always by my side as his spirit leads and directs the path I should take to get out of any of the temptations that I am facing. Keeping in line with God's word daily has helped me shape my spiritual journey and has enabled me to stand firm in the calling of God upon my life.

It's not easy as we are living in a fallen world with Satan knowing that he already lost the battle when Jesus died on the cross for my sins and rose again on the third day to bring salvation to my soul but with that said I await the opportunity when I will be clothed in the spirit of grace and truth to become all that I can be on this side of the world.

There have been times in my life when I feel I cannot make it to the next day because of so much poverty and lack of the basic things which others take for granted but due to faith as small as a seed I am able to pull back and see the hand of God at work miraculously in my situation.

When living in Sierra Leone things were not so favourable as London as there are few opportunities available to secure a risk-free life. This is where my faith in the Lord Jesus plays a great part and by trusting and believing in his word and promises for me, I always come up on top of my situations and see the hand of God at work in my life in every situation I find myself in. It is only by divine encounter that I have been able to make it thus far with the Holy Spirit being my teacher. I had to face up to the challenge but knowing God I am always calm because I know that he will provide and see me through one day at a time with him by my side. Nothing comes by chance, and I have left no stone unturned. I tried to get into the habit of seeking God through prayer and reading the word of God to determine the next way forward in my situation. And God has opened the door for me to live in London after years of trusting and praying for this to happen. Thanks be to God for answering prayers. He keeps on fulfilling his word and I have seen it coming through in my life in every situation I have found myself in. I have wandered away from God, setting my own agenda and doing my own thing but with no satisfaction, only being in God's Kingdom and obeying his voice brings hope and restoration to my soul.

There is nothing bad in my view about God leading me the way to victory in my pursuit of a better lifestyle because he is all-sufficient and has been my Jehovah Jireh since I met him and crowned him Lord of all at the age of 16 years old at the Pentecostal church I was attending, called Bethel Temple in Freetown, Sierra Leone. As with everything I drifted away from the Lord, but his loving arms brought me back to the fold. I did all sorts of shameful acts that I am not proud of, engaged in fornication in which the father of my child told me to have an abortion and he would not be responsible for the care of the child but with a broken heart I decided to go through with the pregnancy and on 24th January 1985 gave birth to a bouncing baby boy at Doctor Culess hospital in Freetown, Sierra Leone. I have a good relationship with my son and it's built-on trust and care for each other and he is the inspiration behind me sharing my story with the outside world. He is my source of strength, and I am encouraged in my journey of life. I thank God that there is forgiveness at the cross of Christ because now I know that it's not about me but his grace that has brought me so far and I know that he will continue to uplift me.

I am soaking myself in God's redeeming love and trying to obey his word through reading the Bible daily. I draw so much encouragement from the Bible and try to apply the teachings of it to my everyday life. The devil is a defeated foe and always looking for an opportunity to attack me either by myself or by someone so dear to me in order to push me off course and to doubt the resurrection power of God, which is at work in my life, but I am hanging there for my victory because God has promised me heaven after this life if I stay faithful to him until the time when he calls me home to glory. I have been battered, torn and rejected by folks, but God's hand of love has reached out to me and he makes me feel accepted in his kingdom.

There is no better way of saying this than to thank the Lord Almighty for his love and mercy which searched me out and established my path to righteousness and Godliness. I am a work in progress as God has not finished with me yet. I am staying on the narrow road that leads to eternal life because there is a lot to be gained from knowing Jesus as my Lord and saviour and I am determined to live a free life from sin and shame. Now I can lift my head up high and thank God once again for his saving grace and for choosing me to be his friend.

I am fascinated in my journey when I am in contact with other people, believers in the faith who share my interest in serving God and try to be all that we can be in our quest to live a successful and righteous life. There are those ones who are short-lived, who try to hinder me from following the truth of the gospel, these ones I try to disengage from and pray that their hearts open to the knowledge of Christ and his power to save.

My circle of friends is small as you can imagine, and I do have few loyal friends who I can count on in these challenging times that I am going through. They have been a shoulder to cry on and have been supportive in my Christian journey. I am honoured to know that they remember me in their prayers daily and I also do the same for them as well. We need each other as Christ also teaches us to go and make disciples of all nations. I do not choose who I befriend, the good Lord brings them to my attention, and I am grateful that they have been much help and assistance in my journey. I can count upon them in everything I encounter, and they will immediately come to my rescue. I have also been able to form friendships in my neighbourhood. It was not like this when I first moved into the area 25 years ago but through prayers daily for God to soften the hearts of the residents, I now have close links in the community. We support each other and we are of help where needed. Sometimes the devil wants to isolate us but through prayers God can change things and bring us together as a community.

I have seen other residents come and go but I am still here making a living and being the best I can be in Jesus Christ's name, amen. It is a very quiet and peaceful area with lots of green trees which I do fancy and it always reminds me of God's creation and his love for the people he has created. There has never been a major issue here with me unlike when I was living at Pullards Hill with crime soaring high over there and I fell victim to its effects I was burgled twice and left with nothing until I secured a place in this area of Wimbledon where I can now live at peace with myself and others around me. It was not a nice experience, I hated every minute I was living in Pullards Hill. It took me 4 years to leave and God in his mercy heard my cry to move and made a way through the crime for me. I have since forgiven the young men involved in the crime and hope to meet Jesus at a certain point in his life and be set free from this evil, which creeps into our society. It is not easy but because I want God to bless me, I believe I must forgive those who did me wrong and release them.

My season of singleness is very productive although I was involved with sex outside marriage and as a result had a son by someone who was so full of himself and does not care about me nor the child, I bore for him. It's heart-breaking to see that I was not supported by him as he stayed away from his responsibilities simply because he was not working at the time, and I was the only one working, at the West African Examinations Council as an accounts clerk. I had to finance all monetary needs of the care for my unborn child and as a single parent see him grow up. At the time of his birth, I was still living at home with my parents although I was working but thanks be to God that he provided a very reasonable boss who took pity on me and helped me in my care responsibilities as far as arranging for childcare whilst I was working.

I am still enjoying my single life now and hoping that one day I will meet my soulmate who has the same beliefs as I have. I pray every day that it is God's will for me to have someone, that the person will show up in my life and not delay coming forward so that together we can plan our future and continue serving God to the best of our abilities.

Nothing is too difficult for our God. He says that we should ask, and it shall be given unto us. He therefore created Adam and Eve for companionship so he who does these things in the world will also bring my helpmate together with me so that we can jointly serve God to the fullest of time in all seasons of life.

I am always asking God for things that I need, and he has been granting my requests though sometimes I have to wait but in the process of waiting I am worshipping and praising God for the results and the desire to get what I have already asked him to give me through talking to him in prayer.

I said to God that I do not want someone who would be irresponsible and may want to use and abuse me. Just send me someone that I am compatible with that we can both share each other's views and live happily thereafter. He is a faithful God and will make a way where there seems to be no way. So, I am currently in the waiting room looking forward to when that need will be met in my life. It is about time things changed for me as I have been unlucky in love. People have used and abused me in the past and that's a horrible feeling to experience when all I want is for someone to share my life with.

I have peace of mind, which only Jesus can give, and I am not in a hurry to get things done. I do work to deadlines but am very careful as to how I go about doing things, for I am cautious so that I do not take the wrong route on my journey and end up on the wrong road, but God has been leading me along the way to victory and I am sure about his loving guidance and care.

Jesus makes all the difference to me, and I know that his leading is always perfect as he directs my path and shows me the way I should go. I do not want to go it all alone but with Jesus in the vessel I am smiling at all the odds that stack up against me. I do see the victory of Jesus in my walk with God as he has been opening doors that seem closed and has also been shutting those doors which I need to close. I am safe in the arms of Jesus, and he is my everything, therefore I lack nothing.

In this season of unemployment that I find myself in he has been making provision for me miraculously and I am also thankful to God for that. I am standing still because I know Jesus personally will take care of my every need.

Chapter 12

Against All Odds

The odds stacked against me are huge but I can overcome each one of them through the power of God and under the guidance of his Holy Spirit bestowed upon me when I first came into the realisation of my need for a saviour to assist me in my quest to live a fulfilling and successful life.

First, I am female which I do admit and quietly take my place in society as a woman living in this world. I do bow down voluntarily to male dominance as this is what I believe God expects of me even in the world of work. I do honour and respect males in my work as I do believe that God created Adam before Eve and as a result as a woman I bow the knee to almighty God in service and reverence to him taking my path well in society.

Then there is the fact that I am a woman of colour. Having been born to African parents I take my race very well as this is intended for me since conception. I was made in the image and likeness of God and carried on and accepting my race for what it is. I know that God did not create me out of chance but by purpose which is ongoing at this present time in history. It has only become a problem for me since I moved over to London in 1998 to live as I have been exposed to all sorts of discrimination in every walk of life, but I have tried to get over the obstacles through the power of good and love confidence in myself and the purpose I am meant to carry out in this world for the benefit of others and God almighty.

Racism has been a problem, but God sees through each one of them through his power. I am therefore counting on the good

Lord to help me overcome all setbacks and continue in the task he has called me to live. Racism and prejudice is due to ignorance so when I am confronted with a racist issue I tend to pray and ask God to forgive them for they know not what they do, they are still in the darkness of life and need to see the light of day to see people of colour as people who are destined for great things in life which God intended for them. The spirit of God tells me to have faith and believe in myself so I now pursue my goals with confidence knowing that God is with me wherever I go, and his presence is evident as I daily seek his will for my life. I try to pursue my life well because the devil will think he is winning the race over my life therefore I give him no reason to overcome me.

Another area of concern to me in my quest to live a fulfilling life here in London is my age. Some may think that I am too old or too young but could get on with any age group. I have been discriminated against by age when some time ago I turned up for a job as a waitress in the restaurant and the owner said to me that they were looking to employ someone who is bright and young but unfortunately I did not fit that group of people. I came back home feeling very sad that I was discriminated against since I was too old. These things happen to me all the time. And, because I do have an English name. Juliet Smith. Employers tend to use this against me, and I have been discriminated against because when I turned up for an interview with British Gas many years ago, they were surprised and shocked to see a black lady by that name coming forward. I was embarrassed as I was asked all sorts of irrelevant questions which had nothing to do with the job I applied for. Out of ignorance people discriminate against me but I don't let that stop me from pursuing my goals in life. I stay positive and actively pursue my God given talent.

I try to let these negative actions by people not get me down nor even negative words spoken about my life that I am not up to anything good because God has a plan, and I am seeking his wise counsel daily to bring it to pass in my life.

If God is for me nothing on earth can be against me because he is the author and finisher of my faith.

Today I can look back and see how far God has brought me from amidst all the trials and tribulations that have surpassed me. When human beings say to me that I am no use in the world, God through his spirit tells me that he has a great plan for me which no one can alter, only by divine intervention will things come to pass according to God's will. So, I continue to rest in his loving care and take the path to holiness and godliness all the days of my life.

I am a chosen one, called to be all that God ordained for me to be in him. He created me and formed me out of the dust of the earth, and I am thankful to him for selecting me above everyone else to serve him in the beauty of his holiness. It is not by chance that I live hand to mouth by God's divine nature. I am who I am in my God. I am ever so grateful for the opportunity given me to serve and live to the best of my ability. I therefore don't let negative situations bring me down because my God is bigger than the troubles I see. He is the rewarder of those who diligently seek him, and he is opening the way to heaven's gate. So, when things don't go as planned, I then turn to God in prayer and commit the whole situation to him and ask him to have his way in it. He is faithful, he has not let me down and never will. It is not in his nature to fail, only my sinful nature leads me not to trust that God will keep his promises.

His ways are just perfect, nothing is hidden from him. He has knowledge of everything in my life and for this I thank him. Sometimes I felt a bit distant from him due to my own faults, but I rise again in faith and continue the journey that is before me to establish my purpose for life.

My journey is not a smooth one because I have been faced with troubles on every side of the way, both great and small, but the presence of the Lord has been with me every step on the way, and I am thankful that Jesus understands me better than anybody else, even my parents don't understand me the way Jesus does. He never fails me and has been reaching out in love towards me ever since I decided to put my trust in him and serve him as my Lord.

When everything is going negatively around me, still there is that calmness I experience from within me assuring me that all will be fine. This is the spirit of God witnessing with my spirit assuring me that God is working everything for my good and all I must do in the given situation is to continue trusting and stay calm and know that God will establish his path to victory on my behalf. When the spirit of God moves within me, I feel certain that God who is all knowing and understands all things will do what he says if only I continue to trust him and live in obedience to his will.

Satan has lost the war in my life as I am totally surrendered to the will of God and no matter what happens to one now or in the future, I will continue to serve the true and living God.

We live in a fallen world with sin taking control of our lives but having sold myself to God's will to allow his spirit to lead me in the way everlasting I am certain that God in his mercy and grace will bring me to an expected end in my desire to be all that God wants me to be. I am surrounded by such lovely people that God brings into my life. They support me and pray for me to be able to live a God-fearing life in the community.

I consult him every day in prayer and his presence goes with me wherever I go. Things are not so rosy but with faith and confidence I rest assured that he will see me through the troubles I face. These are there in order that I might live a successful Christian life geared by the Holy Spirit's prompting. I try to serve my local community the best way possible, and I am guided by God to fulfil his will in my life. No matter what I go through he is the way maker, and he is making his will come to pass in life.

Sometimes I am too impatient with God, having to cut corners to get the job done but being faithful to his calling enables me to overcome all challenges that may come my way and see victory ahead of the struggles. God is so true to his promises, and he sends people along my way to encourage me and help me establish my path to freedom and service to Almighty God. I don't take no for an answer especially when I hear from God that I am in his will. I press forward to the God given goals for my life and continue to seek his divine ordinance and direction. I am also encouraged by others God brings into my life and I continue to uphold such people in my thoughts and prayers. The lockdown that we are experiencing has taught me to be patient and calm, to handle my situation with dignity and caution. Notwithstanding every day brings a different dimension for me and I tend to just go with the flow and not question my God about my current situation but to stand firmly on his word and live one day at a time with the Holy Spirit being my guide.

The spirit leads and shows me the way I should take. Sometimes it's a difficult journey but I have learned to hope in the resurrective power of our Lord and saviour Jesus in those discouraging situations I find myself in. Nothing is by chance but by divine instructions from above. I focus on the cross for my direction and God has been my help in ages past over the years of my existence.

There are wounds which need to be healed by the spirit of God and I await his hand of healing upon my life as I continue to trust that he will carry me through and bring me to victory and deliverance from the physical and spiritual hurts I am currently experiencing. God is indeed opening the door to heaven's gate and is refreshing my mind every moment of the day as I seek to continue to have faith in his word and do his bidding while the time is within my reach. God makes everything possible and is constantly meeting my every need as I continue to give myself to his will and guidance.

It is not an easy road because this world is broken with sin due to the disobedience of our forefathers Adam and Eve. Nothing is out of reach and total confidence and surrender to his will to make everything a plan. I am not suggesting that things are perfect here on earth for me but saying that because we live in a fallen world everything needs to be in total submission to the will of God if ever we are to see the light at the end of the tunnel and see victories which have already been worn at the cross for humanity. Therefore, despite my situation I am confident that God will continue to hold me in his loving arms and guide and direct me in the path I should follow.

It is with a heavy heart that we lose some and we gain some, but whichever way things happen I am resting in God's love and tender care and mercy for my life. I have lost several people in my life due to death over the years and I have learned to trust and rely on God for the way forward to tackle my grief. It is not easy but with God's power he is seeing me through all the challenges of life that I face. Only Jesus can satisfy my longing to serve and honour him all the days of my life and I am happy to be chosen by him to live my life in the fullness of his spirit guiding me.

There have been times when I have felt lonely and bored with the whole concept of life in general, but his loving arms are surrounding me and enabling me to feel the warmth of his embrace. Only faith in the Lord Jesus can do such a thing for me and I am grateful to God for sending Jesus to rescue me from all my fears and boredom. God uses situations to humble me and brings out the best of my personality, therefore I try to ask God to tell me what road I should take and how best I can help in those distressing and difficult situations I find myself in. I feel torn between two walls being pulled here and there. This is where prayer works and when I surrender to his will, he brings everything to pass, and I then see that indeed God is working in it all to make his name precious in my life because I will end up giving him the glory when I have overcome the obstacles that I face.

My boredom is due to the fact that when I take my eyes of Jesus then things go in the opposite direction than I want them to go but as soon as I come back to my senses and say Lord over to you in surrender and worship then he instils my life with peace and love and joy in the Holy Spirit and everything becomes so real to me that I end up regretting not trusting him for his grace and mercy earlier.

The battle with the flesh and the spirit is a war which is going on until Christ comes back or until I die, therefore I do not take things for granted. I rely on the Holy Spirit these latter years to sustain me and fill me anew with his love and mercy. The gift of God has been bestowed upon me and I am using it every day in prayer and worship to almighty God. It is only by the grace of God that I am because I do not deserve to be alive this day to see the goodness of the Lord in the land of the living. Only his divine love has spared my life to be counted among the living and for this I worship and praise his name for the opportunity to enter the holiest of holies.

My mind is sometimes weak due to being led astray by sin but God's power within me enables me to overcome the control of sin and come back to God in repentance and assurance of faith in God. There are times that I do enjoy good times when my spirit is lifted high, and I feel able to face anything that comes my way whether good or bad but there are other times when I feel down and sad due to something negative that recently occurred in my life. This is when the spirit comes to me and assures me of God's love for my life. I am very thankful to him for this.

I face the devil with God's spirit, which resides with me and tells me that nothing is too difficult for my God to deliver me from. Having the confidence and grace to wait upon him in prayer and worship enables me to see my way forward and see the victory ahead of me. He has never failed me yet and never will because it is not in his nature to fail. He always keeps his word and brings his promises to life in my life. My walk with God is sweet and pleasant and I just keep falling in love with him repeatedly. There is no better friendship I have with God than his spirit which enables me to live life in its fullness.

I live in the presence of the Lord and am ruled by his spirit daily to help me in my time of need. I have been sold to Jesus; he has bought me with his precious blood when he died at the cross of Calvary to bring salvation to my soul. I am indeed grateful to God for this and will continue to walk in the newness of life because the life I now live in the flesh is by the grace of God and nothing of my doings that all this is being made possible. My demand to Satan is 'keep your hands of my life I am a child of God, redeemed, saved, and satisfied by his precious blood which was shed for me many years ago.' I now live in fullness of my calling and serve God and my community.

Another area of me being subjected to negative words spoken over my life is at the world of work where I had to endure challenges based on my religion. I quickly concluded that the person who made the negative comment towards me was trying to bring me down as she has no religion at all. The most depressing issue of it was that she was the same colour as me. I was heartbroken but I had to let it slip over me as there were more important things in life that one needed to consider and at the end of the day people are people. Some will favour you, but others will disagree with you for whatever reason they may have.

She made the negative comment in the presence of other staff members to seek approval. I kept silent about the matter when suddenly, the superior approached me to find out how I was feeling about the remarks she made. I told him that I was fine and sometimes these things do happen. We seek a kingdom which is not of this world and Jesus himself told us that we will be persecuted for the gospel's sake so we must not lose heart but continue serving and trusting God to see us through one day at a time with our God. In fact, this is not the first instance people, so-called unbelievers of the gospel, have commented and said all kinds of negative things about my faith in the Lord Jesus, but I do not let it deter me from following Jesus all the way to eternity. Wherever I go or serve, people can truly spot the difference in my life and ask me the reason for the hope that I found in Christ. I thank God for the opportunity to share about the good news of salvation to others so that they too will see the light of day and put their trust in God.

Another place I worked at was the White House, as a Support Worker looking after people with learning difficulties, some of whom also present with challenging needs. It is a hard job going to work every day. Only God's hand of love was helped me through the days' tasks as I always prayed and committed the whole work to him in prayer.

There was a service user who is called Christopher who was very difficult to manage. No one wanted to be his key worker and he was left alone without having any key worker for a while, but the manager said to me 'I think that you get on well with Christopher because whenever you are on duty he tends to behave and talks kindlier about you when you are off duty so why can't you be his key worker.' It was a role I took on voluntarily and both of us got on well with each other. These things were only achievable due to the power of prayer and committing every day to God in prayer for sustenance.

I don't give up on anyone; if God loves them so do I. I am always available to serve my community to the best of my abilities with the help of the Holy Spirit who makes all things beautiful. People come across with various attributes and I try to get along with each other no matter what the situation that I find myself in. I trust that God will see me through each day's tasks and at the end of it all be pleased with myself that I have done a good job. So, if people pick on me for whatever reason I rest my case to almighty God to fight my battles for me and give me victory in the end.

I am always grateful to God because my life as a believer in the Lord Jesus Christ speaks well to others who are curious to know about the hope I have in God and why I am so calm amidst all the troubles that surround me. I put it down to the fact that God is in the storms of my life, and he is the one who oversees my life. I am just a passenger in the car, and he takes the wheel and leads me onto where he wants me to go and all I do is to follow his lead with the help of the Holy Spirit who is at work in my life. Some people think that because I am kind, calm and quiet they can just walk all over me and take advantage of my generous nature, but I have learned not to put up a fight but to commit everything to God in prayer.

God has been helping me to have a common purpose for living ever since I decided to put my trust in him. He leads me to higher ground of victory, and I just see the mercy and favour come to pass in my life and that brings courage in a world filled with sin and shame. I am left to thank God for the good work he is currently doing in my life and to continue serving him and others the best way possible, which is within my reach.

I know God will not give me a burden that I cannot carry so whatever comes my way I rest assured that he will hold me in his grips and will not let me wander from his arms ever again. I have come a long way with my service unto the Lord and I see what he has done in my life, and I surrender to his will daily to continue to create within me a heart full of praise and adjuration to him. I don't let people's negative words spoken about my life deter me from getting my blessings from God because this is what Satan wants. I press on and keep on holding onto the truth of God's word and try to live a faithful life for his glory. It is all praise to God wo makes all this possible and my total willingness to obey his word and apply it to my life. I am not perfect, but I am striving for perfection because Jesus commands his followers to be perfect.

I am an introvert. I like to spend time at home a lot; my home is my castle. I have developed a certain routine of life which I pursue at home to bring out the best of me. I can stay home all week without going out and that suits me perfectly well. But sometimes I think I need to be out in the open to get some fresh air and see people going about their normal duties. I am satisfied with my routine and continue to minister to my needs daily, and that of others as well, whom God brings along the way. I am trying to read the Bible with the help of the Word for Today guidelines and it is fascinating to read the scriptures that God brings to my attention. I am following the guideline daily to read the entire Bible within the year. This is a great challenge I have set for myself, and I am trusting God to make this all possible within the given time. I like peace and quiet and I am lucky to live in an area that just fulfils that need in my life so that I can focus on God more and pray regularly and commit the needs of myself and others to him in prayer. There are lots of lessons I am learning from the Bible which I am applying to my daily life so that I will become a much better Christian living on earth.

In every circumstance of life, I have learned to trust in Jesus and to apply the word of God in my life. I try to do what the scriptures tell me to do after praying over the situation asking for the Holy Spirit to lead and direct my life. It is not possible only to hear the word of God preached if we don't apply the word to our daily life and draw strength from it. This is where the Holy Spirit helps me in my weakness because sometimes I am too lazy to get things done but when the spirit prompts me to take action I then throw myself up and do what I have to do in order to be at peace with God. The Holy Spirit is a great teacher as he teaches me the truth of the gospel and shows me the way I should take in each situation.

Jesus did not leave me alone but led me to seek his comfort to help me in all areas of my life. He teaches, instructs, guides me in the way everlasting and I am grateful to God for sending him to my life to put the record straight. Without God and the Holy Spirit I am lost in this world, but thanks be to God that he answers my troubled prayer and assists me in my desire to serve him fully. I am very happy that I know God and Jesus Christ is my saviour who has rescued me from sin and shame no matter what the devil tells me.

There is a need to pursue some tasks that are dear to my heart and in keeping with the schedule of life. I tend to accomplish a lot of things to the glory of God. My daily mission is to let others get the most out of life's chances and survive the hardship which may deter them from fulfilling their potential in God.

I like to be a shoulder to cry on and help others ascertain certain criteria that meet everyday standards of living through the prayers and help of a support network of believers. I can see God transform and uplift me to further the work I am here to do on earth. Things have not been easy as there are setbacks along the way but with the dedication of my friends and fellow Christians in the Lord, I am able to see God move in my life like never before and see miracles happen before my naked eyes.

I have been unwell for some time with a hip injury, and I have been unable to perform tasks that I usually do but with prayers and support from my team and health professionals I am now fully recovered, all down to lots of prayers said on my behalf. I give thanks to God for his hand of healing upon my life and the love showed by Christians.

I do have scars in my life that remind me of God's goodness and mercy towards me and that of the people who are so dear to me. I have been bruised, bombarded by negative actions that sometimes caused me to doubt my own existence upon the earth and the reason behind it all. But having been in contact with the right people, I mean people who know their God, I am left to consider my ways and run to the heaven of safety swiftly.

This is where the spirit of God does some real planning in my life and gives me the assurance that I am not alone, as God is always with me every step of the way. My experiences I have been through were bitter and bad, not being able to trust family members again who took advantage of me and abused me because they were seen as the most powerful personality in our family circle. That is why I am saying these things, so that help will come sooner rather than later. I didn't think I can trust any human being again after such horrendous happenings. I have bounced back, ready to go. No matter what has happened to me I am still confident that my God is able to set me free and release me from the control of evil and wicked people.

I have had my own share of hardship in both worlds that I have lived in. Firstly, the economic situation in Sierra Leone left me feeling so disconnected from the outside world. There are times when we just did not have food to eat and the shoes I had on as a child were all worn out not fit for habitation and I was faced with no electricity and scarcely any food or water but to the glory of God I was able to see God make provision for me and my family as I do believe in prayer and the power of God at work when we call upon him in a desperate situation. My only hope was to escape from that kind of upbringing and come back to London to make a living and be set free from the circumstances that made me unhappy and to doubt the power of God which is at work in my life.

But God was ever so faithful, he kept his promises to me and always supplied my needs. I am saying this because God is the provider of my every need, and he made a way where it seemed impossible to survive the hard times that I faced, but as the saying goes 'where there is life there is hope'.

When I talk about hardship, Jesus did not promise me that life would be a bed of roses because we live in a fallen world every here on earth is broken. Things are never right, there's always trouble from every corner of the universe waging war on my existence but having confidence and trust in the God who created me and knowing me fully through and through I am left with no option than to continue living and trusting God that he will see me through the various obstacles and barriers I may face in life.

And I am thankful to God that he has measured me up to his standard and as special person in his family of God and no matter how the enemy desires to distract me, I am certain that God in his holiness will deliver me and see me through one step at a time. God is preserving me from all the attack of Satan and his foes as I have learned to trust him for his grace and favour. No two days are the same, one day I am up and about and other days I just want to take things slowly and relax at home praying and asking God to help me get my foot finally on the ground and live a successful life.

I am at this present time recovering from an injured hip which affected my thighs and right knee. They have been very painful; I have been taking pain killers and other medication to ease the pain with no success until I started doing some physio exercises having been referred by my doctor to the physiotherapist. I am fully recovered from this, an experience which I do not want to let repeat itself, never again in the future. It took me 3 months, doing the exercises nearly every day for 40 minutes until I saw improvement in my health. During this time, I was in deep conversation with God about it, seeking my healing and deliverance in this matter, but God's timing is always perfect and in his own time he sent help and assistance. In fact, I had to discontinue taking pain killers because I was nauseous and the doctor said that I will have no more options because there were only a few medicines I could take as I am suffering from high blood pressure and the doctor can't just prescribe me anything in this situation. But I have a God who is my healer to pray fervently to daily and I was also privileged to have others who prayed for me, I was able to do well and get on with other things like starting a new job, which I am enjoying.

I am only pulling through life's journey by exercising faith in God and allowing him to do the work of life in my journey so far with him. It is not easy but one thing I know is that God is with me every step of the way holding me in his hands and preparing me for the journey I am taking. Only by his grace I am what I am today, satisfied and determined to be always in his will.

Sometimes the pressure of life overwhelms me and causes me to doubt his power, but the spirit of God is faithful and tells me to trust in God for my victory. So, no matter what life throws at me I am rest assured that my days of abundance and plenty will soon be here for all the world to see, that I am indeed serving the true and living God who provides for his children, and I am one of them. There was no one I can talk to concerning my problems within my family as the culprits were respected members of the family. I only talked to God in prayer and poured my heart out to him for deliverance and assurance that I would be fine. No one in my family would believe me, they will think I was just making it up, but God knows the truth of the whole matter and came to my rescue when I needed the help

It is not always possible to get on top of your situations, especially when foes are a bit negative and do not give the right kind of advice and help that is needed. But seeking God through prayers enables me to overcome all trials and setbacks that confront me. I am very grateful to God for coming through for me in times when I am down and out, not thinking right and at times falling into sin because of me not yielding correctly to the voice of the Holy Spirit which aids me in my walk of life as I am truly a servant of the highest God.

God is in the business of sorting me out as I am a work in progress. He has not finished the work in me yet, still ploughing onto victory as everyday sees a very different trend to my integration in the society in which I belong. He is seeing me through one day at a time by his grace and mercy. I have come to depend upon his actions and provisions for my life as I truly seek to please and serve him whole heartedly.

I have learnt in recent years to always offer communication with God and in all situations of life that I find myself in, both for myself and the peoples of the universe. In fact, I pray to God ever so often and in all places that I find myself in. The good thing about this spiritual exercise is that God comes through for me in answering my prayers and answering my request each time I call upon him, so this makes me glad and assured that I have someone in the heavens who meets me at the point of my needs.

I excel because of my confidence in God, knowing that he is always near when I am upset or when negative emotions overwhelm me. I can always count on his divine assistance. He makes me happy and glad that I can trust him for he never fails and will minister and help me out in all areas of life that I face. Each time I feel that things are not right with me and suffer from negative emotions I tend to take a step back and pray to God to assist me in my need to be able to move forward in the light of a positive encounter with the world I live in. It is always helpful to read the Bible to help me focus on my need for acceptance and assurance in my faith as a Christian as I can see how other people in the Bible times have made if in their time did when confronted with disaster of whatever sort.

There are people God placed in my life to assist me when life gets too much to bear. These are people I can count on as they have always been a shoulder to cry on. They have been there for me through thick and through thin. My church family members have been supportive of me in advising and praying for me when issues come up and I am thankful to God that I belong to a church that cares for me and helps me to be all I am in God.

They have been encouraging me and helping me to be integrated in society. I don't know what I would do if I did not have this body of Christ behind me to assist, pray and empower me in all areas of my life.

My Tuesday Bible study group members are particularly helpful. I am not ashamed or fearful to tell the group when we do meet about things that stand in the way of my life. They have rendered practical help as well. I gain hope by reading the Bible every day and allowing God to speak to me, spending time in a very peaceful and quiet atmosphere.

Satan got me hooked up in gambling, betting daily until it was leading to financial strain so much so that I accrued rent arrears of £5,000. The council took me to court for non-payment of the rent. Only after contacting Christians Against Poverty, who then contacted my church Emmanuel church, Wimbledon, who were very kind enough to pay the money owed, was I able to continue living in my house. All thanks and praise to God that the church could step up to confront such a negative thing on my part. Since then, I have been able to quit gambling and pay all my bills as and when they are due. If it was not for the fact that the church stepped in, I would have been homeless by now. But I am thankful that God made a way where there seemed to be no way for me and now I am a living proof that love and care surrounds God's people.

I was able to make a budget which I am following up to this day and sticking to the plan. I owe it all to my church family to seek and serve in whatever way I can because they have been there for me when I have needed help and support. The assurance is overwhelming indeed.

I do feel tempted now and again, but I try to resist the urge and try to make my money work for me instead of giving it over to the devil in this way because God is so good to me, and he is seeking the best way for me to manage my finances in a more positive and refined manner. It could have been worse but thankfully help came sooner rather than later and today I can talk about my experience in this matter.

We are not perfect; only fools think that they have arrived. Jesus came for a sinner like me, and I am not ashamed to tell my story as it happened because I have a testimony at the end of it and know that God has been there for me through it all.

Now I try to support good causes by making a donation where the need arises. In this way I am storing up treasures in heaven and fulfilling the gospel's message to do good to all humans as good has been done to me as well. To repay the good by helping others get a bright start in life and therefore obey the commandments of God to love one another and I can say that the best way of doing that is in the act of giving.

No donation is too small. I pray fully to consider how much to give and then send it straight away from my bank. There are lots of needs around these days and only God can tell me who to support in my finances because I do not want to be disobedient to God but to do his will in my life always and that is also true of my financial area as well. And since I have considered this venture, God has been a blessing to me so much so that I cannot, tell if in all his goodness and mercy he has bestowed on me tiny things; like picking up leftovers from the supermarket and paying a bit cheaper for groceries. I am grateful to God for every blessing I get because if it were not for his love for me and my obedience to his commands none of these would ever happen. I put myself in the position where God can use me fully, withholding nothing but being willing and available to be used by God in all situations I face in life. I have learned in whatsoever state I am in to be content and pray, seeking God to help me in my weakness to be strong and abide by his laws as laid out in the Bible, which is the guide that directs and empowers me in my service to the Lord. I have a sense of belonging now having a partnership with God.

My inner circle is a bit small. I have few people I can relate to when I need to talk about anything that pertains to my welfare. These are my close contacts and they have been supportive to me over the years. We get along well and I can count on them when I do need the help. They have been my good friends and believers in the Lord, praising for me and advising me in any issues I face in a God-fearing manner. I don't know what I will do if these two people are not in my life. Only God knows it all. We stayed in touch with each other over the years. In fact, one of them, Saliane Campbell, is God mother to my son Jenner. She has been a shoulder to cry on and I thank God for bringing us together in his love. We both happen to be born in the same month of July and therefore have the same qualities in our lives. She is someone I can trust as she has proved herself strong in my life over the years. We have really come a long way in our socialisation process and have grown up in the Lord over this set time. Saliane is someone I can trust and appreciate. There is always a smile each time I see her.

My dad was a strict disciplinarian, very stern but loving as well. He showed no favourites to us his children. There are four of us in our family, myself and three others and also an outside child from another woman, making us five on my dad's side whilst four on my mum's side.

My mum showed favourites in that she showed care and more attention to my brother Victor and Audrey my sister because they were the two youngest in the family. I never experienced the love of my mother, she was always condemning and criticising me for everything I did. I tried to get a motherly love from others outside the family, who showed me love and respect and helped me to be successful in what I chose to do in life. It was a heart-breaking experience for me, I tried to secure the appreciation and love of my mother, but she was never there for me. In fact, when she came to London on holidays from Sierra Leone many years ago, on her return I bought some clothing for my son so she could take them to him for me and give to him, as he was then living with his dad, but she went and sold the clothing and spent the money on herself. Can you imagine how cruel that is to your own grandchild?

In my secondary school education, I was lucky enough to have a scholarship from the City Council in Freetown Sierra Leone whilst attending the Methodist Girls High School until I finished school in 1979 and passed the GCSE 'O' level exams. I was an above average student, having excelled in French during my school days and obtaining prizes in French in a few schools academic years awards.

I loved French so much and was getting on well with my teacher Monsieur Gavin but unfortunately I did not pursue that line of action on finishing school. All the French I learnt then went to waste. Not knowing that God had other plans for my life I came to London in 1988 and in 1993 studied Social Sciences (Gender Studies) at Kingston University. I was hoping to become a social scientist with that but plans again did not work out as I was ill whilst studying for the final exam. On recovering from that spell of depression I gave up the idea of taking the exam and tried to look for something else when I began working as a Support Worker at a care home. Problems with a resident accusing me of theft forced me to leave that employment.

There have been a series of bad occurrences in my quest to be able to live a rewarding and fulfilling life in society, but thanks be to God that he sees and feels my pain and the fact that I can move on in life in a more positive sphere makes it all the more worthwhile.

I just cannot break free, I keep going in circles of life like Jonah in the Bible. Spending three days and nights in the fish belly. Mine is more than that. I spent years round the bend with no way out until I trusted and asked upon God's word that he would make a way for me out of my desolate situation. Only God can help me, therefore I need to put myself in a position where I hear from him and obey his words in my life. He promises me good will come out of my situation if I focus upon him and take him at his word. That's what I am doing now. If people including family members are negative to me yet I know I can trust the one who hopes my future and who will see me through the various tests and needs that I have. I have always been afraid of the dark ever since I was a child growing up. Darkness even now frightens me. I dread the winter months.

I will never forget the encounter I had with Jesus during the time I was watching a film in my local church called Bethel Temple, in Freetown. The film was entitled Thief in the Night. I was so much afraid of being cut up in the affairs of being left behind if I did not accept Jesus Christ as my Lord and saviour. I was full of fears and confessed my follies there and then and made a commitment to follow Jesus' teachings and become a part of the family of God. Since I was 16 years old, I never looked back on that decision. It actually paid off, all my hopes and fears were banished, and I became a new person unto whom justice seeks for the lost and dying. Now I pray ever so often and present the needs of myself and others before the throne room of God.

I am very fascinated at the many prayers that God has answered in this capacity. God loved to hear me call upon myself in all spheres of life, whether happy or sad. He means everything to me, I cannot live without him and he is the reason I am alive because he stepped into my world when I swallowed a needle and did what was necessary to get it out of my body.

Perseverance is the key to my development in this life that I am living to the full. Nothing comes by chance, I must make every opportunity useful and take steps to bring it to pass on a daily basis with a bit of care and attention to detail. I am persuaded that my life is now heading in the right direction to bring more glow and Sundance in my walk with the Lord. Every challenge is there to bring me to a perfect conclusion, and I am happy to say that my life has really struck a positive note of trust and care in the Lord.

Every battle is a way to see the fullness of God at work in my life. I am happy for the outcome as I seek to serve and honour my creator all the days of my life. I am therefore not at logger heads with the behaviours of some folks who think that I am just forcing my way in the circumstances I face, not adjusting well to sort out my troubles.

Therefore, only a handful of people I can say have been a shoulder to cry on when things have not been favourable for me. I never had an easy life. In fact, life has been tough, rough, and unbearable but with the help from God I am able to overcome all challenges.

My greatest achievement is when I gave birth to my son Jenner Stronge on 24 January 1985. My partner then was not so keen on the idea, but I was left with no choice than to go through with the pregnancy and today me and my son are good friends, we get along well, and I can confide to him on whatever issues are facing me at that moment.

In fact, it's his idea for me to write my story so that the world may know about me and all that has happened to me in my life. I owe it to myself and I am also thankful for the gift of a son who also has accepted Jesus Christ as his Lord and saviour and is living in obedience to his will.

He has the fear of God within himself. He understands me more than anybody does, and I am bestowed upon him to nurture and care for him until he finds his way in life on his own because he has since moved house and is now living on his own.

My dream job was to become a policewoman. I tried to apply for the role but was unsuccessful in the selection process as I failed the medical and they were looking for people who were fit and healthy. Even though that did not materialise yet, I continued to pursue other employments that would welcome me in the labour market. I succeeded in some although a few of them were for a short space of time, since I was unhappy with work settings and the wages were not so good as well. But nevertheless, I tried to put my head above waters and keep afloat in my desire to pursue my goals to make a living for myself and my son as I was also a single parent.

Jenner is now 36 years old, and he loves to care for dogs as a means of earning a bit of cash. He is very good with these dogs. I sometimes help him out by looking after them when the need arises, for when asked to do that and I find that they are indeed man's best friend. They are loving creatures that brighten the day. When my mother failed to be there for me through thick and thin, I relied on Jenner's wise counsel to support me and help me overcome my struggles. He is such an adorable young man who loves God with his heart and is also helping others that God brings along his path. I am just lucky to have him around me all the time and I am thrilled to have seen him grow up over the years.

When things do not seem right, I like to pour out my heart before God and trust in prayer asking him to sort things out for me and help me to get on with the task for the day. Therefore, I take one day at a time, prayerfully going through all tasks that I need to accomplish as the day wears on. There is sometimes not enough time in the day to get all these sorts of things done, but with the help from above I am able to do the most I can in all areas of my life and leave everything to God to work it all out for my benefit. It is all about getting the balance right with rest and play and determining when I should stop or move forward in each task. I try to minimize stress a lot because I can easily be stressed out if I am not careful with things. I try to let God move me on, rather than me moving things on my own effort. I need that push from on high and certainly that God will bring me out victoriously to overcome all challenges that I may face. As the days go by, I see God's hand of love reaching out to me and helping me to take the initiative to move onto a better life in him and be successful.

I try to tell myself not what society wants me to be or what other people want me to be either. I am taking life slowly but surely with God by my side and the Holy Spirit assisting me and guiding me in the way everlasting. So now that things are moving on nicely for me, I am thankful that God is the one who makes all this possible and I would like to take this chance to praise God for all the good work he is doing in my life. Without him I am lost in the desert with no one to talk to or to assist me to find my way back in life.

Thanks also to God for the gift of prayer and worship which is a part of my daily routine. God's hands are upon me, making straight my rough life and bringing me to a safe haven of rest in the one whom I serve, that is God almighty. God promises me that he will make a way for me where there seems to be no way and if only I can see him at work in my life then I will have no other way than to thank him very much for all his loving kindness towards me and my family who care for me.

Poverty attached itself to me but not for too long because I have a God I serve who provides for my every need. He always makes a way for me, whenever I call upon his name. He has been good to me over the years, doing me favours at cost and in all situations. The need to have it all is ongoing, but I am still trusting God to make me live a fulfilling and settled life in the society to which I belong.

I can now see God's hands at work in my life daily as I pursue my God given talents and use my skills and gifts for his glory. There is always a new beginning now and again and I am grateful that God is there beside me whenever I need him most. He sustains me and takes active care of my everyday life. I am so happy to be chosen to be part of what God is doing in this part of the world in which I live. I appreciate him for his care and daily provision. I can now boast in his power and might, as I be strong then with help from above. There are times in my life when God remains silent, I am reaching out to him, but he seems too distant from me and I wonder why he left me in suspense and did not heed my cry but silence usually means that God is still working in the process of time to manifest his will.

In those situations of my development, I try to figure out what \I can be doing while waiting for God to act upon my behalf. Sometimes I spend time in praise, worship, and thanksgiving because he sees all things and will come through for me if I do not give up and continue worshipping and using his name in my situation.

It's hard going as I don't know what to expect but since I am serving a God who understands I trust and take him at his word, firmly declaring the promises of God upon my life. That is why I spend time reading the Bible daily and am familiar with the promises of God. The advice I take on board is to always allow God to rule and direct my life because he knows what is best for my life and he will make all things work for my God if I let him take the driving seat of my lie. It is not always easy to let him rule in my life as the devil seeks to devour me but I have hope in God and what he can do for me makes it all the easier. I face challenges in my journey of life every now and then but the most important thing is that these setbacks have helped to shape my life and have given me a new lease of life as I seek to answer him more and be obedient to his voice as he speaks to me daily.

I do not allow people or situations to bring me down in life. I know who I am, and I am able to pursue all the goals and tasks set before me on a daily basis. I do not yield to negative speaking over my life because God has made me to be real and genuine in my quest to be integrated in this side of the world. I live in some discrimination from people who don't see things the way I do get into the ways of me and my God. He has created me for a purpose and that is to serve him and to be in his kingdom rule. God is my centre of attraction and I got confidence in his divine care and attention upon my life. Jesus is the author and finisher of my faith, and it gives me so much joy to know that Jesus can sort out my worries if I allow him in my life and crown him Lord and saviour.

I know that better days are ahead of me, and I wait upon God to move in my life as I seek to please him in all that I do in this world. I have no other helper except God on his throne in heaven, he sees and satisfies every longing in my life. I am also very glad because a higher power is at my request when I need that push in the right direction.

Sometime ago when I was going through a period of depression and didn't know what to do with my life, I suddenly realised the hand of God was reaching out to me in love and bringing me out of that state of ill health and restoring my life to full fellowship with him. I have since then been stable on medication and it's all praise and thanks to God who heals all my sickness. The journey of my health is so raw with lots of moaning about why and how I came to suffer from this illness.

I put it down to stress and the university workload I was pursuing at that time, somewhere around 1993, which made me to be unable to take my final exam at university. All is not lost as I am slowly getting things sorted and wait patiently for the red lights to pursue other avenues that are of interest to me.

I was admitted on two occasions to hospital for this illness because I refused to take medication and was in total denial of the condition, but I then finally realised that if I admit the fact that I am ill and take the medication prescribed I would be able to recover from it very quickly. This I have done ever since I decided to own up to my sickness.

Chapter 13

Endure, Hardship and Pain

I have had my own share of hardship in both worlds that I have lived with.

Firstly, the economic situation in Sierra Leone left me feeling so disconnected from the outside world. There were times when we just did not have food to eat and the shoes I had on as a child were all worn out, not fit to be worn, and I was faced with no electricity and scarcely any food and water but to the glory of God I was able to see God make provision for me and my family as I do believe in prayer and the power of God at work when we call upon him in desperate situations. My only hope then was to escape from that kind of upbringing, come back to London to make a living and be set free from the circumstances that make me unhappy, and also free from doubt in the power of God which is at work in my life.

But God was ever so faithful, he kept his promises to me and always supplied for my needs. I am saying this because God is the provider of my every need, and he has made a way where it all seems impossible to survive the hard times that I faced.

When I talk about hardship Jesus did not promise me that life would be a bed of roses because we live in a fallen world everything here on earth is broken. Things are never right, there is always trouble from every corner of the universe raging war on my existence but having confidence and trust in the God who created me and knowing me fully through and through, I am left with no option than to continue living and trusting that God will see me through the various obstacles and corners I may face in life.

And I am thankful to God that he has measured me up to his standard as a royal priest and special person in his family. I have been adopted to the family of God and though the enemy tries to distract me I am certain that God in his holiness will deliver me and see me through one step at a time. God is preserving me from all the attacks of Satan and his foes, and I have learned to trust him for his grace and favour. No two days are the same, one day I am up and about, and other days I just want to take things slowly and relax at home praying and asking God to help me get my foot firmly on the ground and live a successful life.

I am at this present time recovering from an injured hip which affected my thighs and right knee. They have been very painful. I have been taking pain killers and other medication to ease the pain but there was no success until I started doing some physio exercises having been referred by my doctor to the physiotherapist. I am fully recovered from this, an experience which I do not want to let repeat itself ever again. It took me several months doing the exercises nearly every day for 40 minutes until I could see an improvement in my health. During this time, I have been in deep conversation with God about it, seeking my healing and deliverance in this matter, but God's living is always perfect, in his own time he sent help and assistance. In fact, I had to discontinue taking pain killers because I was nauseous, and the doctor says that I will have no more options because there were only a few medicines I could take as I am suffering from high blood pressure and can't just prescribe anything in this situation. But I have a God who is my healer, having prayed fervently to him daily and I was also privileged to have others who prayed for me. I was able to get well and get on with other things like starting a new job that I am enjoying.

I am only pulling through life's journey by exercising faith in God and allowing him to do the work of life in my journey so far with him. It's not easy but one thing I know is that God is with me every step of the way, holding me in his hands and preparing me for the journey I am taking only by his grace. I am what I am today, sealed satisfied and determined to be always in his will. Sometimes the pressure of life overwhelms me and causes me to doubt his power, but the spirit of God is faithful and tells me to trust in God for my victory. So, no matter what life throws at me I am rest assured that my days of abundance and plenty will soon be here for all the world to see that I am indeed serving the true and living God who provides for his children, and I am one of them.

It's not always possible to come over the top of your situations, especially when foes are a bit negative and do not give the right kind of advice and help that's needed. But seeking God through prayer enables me to overcome all trials and setbacks that confront me. I am grateful to God for coming through for me in times when I am down and out, not thinking right and at times falling into sin as a result of me not yielding correctly to the voice of the Holy Spirit which aides me in my walk of life as I am truly a servant of the highest God. God is in the business of sorting me out as I am a work in progress. He has not finished the work in me yet, still ploughing on to victory as everyday sees a very different trend to my integration in the society in which I belong. He is seeing me through one day at a time by his grace and mercy. I came to depend upon his actions and provisions for my life as I truly seek to please and serve him wholeheartedly.

I have learnt in recent years to always offer a communication with God and in all situations of life that I find myself in both for myself and the people of the universe. In fact, I pray to God ever so often and in all places that I find myself in. The good thing about this spiritual exercise is that God comes through for me in answering my prayers and acts on my request each time I call upon him, so this makes me glad and assured that I have someone in the heavens who meets me at the point of my needs.

I excel because of my confidence in God, knowing that he is always near when I am upset or when negative emotions overwhelm me. I can always count on his divine assistance. He makes me happy and glad that I can trust him for he never fails and will minister and help me out in all areas of life that I face. Each time I feel that things are not right with me and I am suffering from negative emotions, I tend to take a step back and pray to God to assist me in my need to be able to move forward in the light of a positive encounter with the world I live in. It's always helpful to read the Bible to help me focus on my need of acceptance and assurance in my faith as a Christian as I can see how other people in Biblical times made it when confronted with disaster of whatever sort it was.

There are people God has placed in my life to assist me when life gets too much to bear. These are people I can count on as they have always been a shoulder to cry on. They have been there for me through thick and through thin. My church family members have supported me in advising and praying for me when issues have come up and I am thankful to God that I belong to a church that cares for me and helps me to be all I am in God. They have been encouraging me and helping me to be integrated in society.

I do not know what I can do if I do not have this body of Christ behind me to assist, pray and empower me in all areas of my life. My Tuesday Bible Study Group members are particularly helpful where I am not ashamed or fearful to tell the group when we do meet about things that stand in the way of my life. They have rendered practical help as well and pray also that now I see that in all this God was there bringing people to my rescue. I hope by reading the Bible every day and allowing God to speak to me and I can spend time in a very peaceful and quiet atmosphere.

I am very fascinated at the many prayers that God has answered on behalf of myself and others. God loves to hear me call upon me in all spheres of life, whether happy or sad. He means everything to me. I cannot live without myself, and he is the reason I am alive because he stepped into my world when I swallowed a needle and did what was necessary to get it out of my body.

Perseverance is the key to my development in this life that I am living to the full. Nothing comes by chance; I must make every opportunity useful and take steps to bring it to pass daily with a bit of care and attention to detail. I am persuaded that my life is now heading in the right direction to bring more glow and substance in my walk with the Lord. Every challenge is there to bring me to a perfect conclusion, and I am happy to say that my life has really turned into a positive note of trust in the Lord. Every battle is a way to see the fullness of God at work in my life.

I am happy for the outcome as I seek to serve and honour my creator all the days of my life. I am therefore no longer ends with the behaviours of some folks who think that I am just forcing my way in the circumstances I face not advising me well to sort out my troubles. Therefore, only a handful of people I can say have been a shoulder to cry on when things are not favourable for me. I never had an easy life. In fact, life has been tough, rough and unbearable but with the help from God I am able to overcome all challenges.

My greatest achievement was when I gave birth to my son Jenner Stronge on 24th January 1985. My partner then was not so keen on the idea, but I was left with no choice than to go through with the pregnancy and today me and my son are good friends. We get along well, and I can confide to him on whatsoever issues that is facing me at that moment. In fact, it's his idea for me to write my story so that the world may know about me and all that has happened to me in my life

My dream job was to become a policewoman. I tried to apply for the role but was unsuccessful in the selection process as I failed the medical and they were looking for people who were fit and healthy. Even though that did not materialise yet, I continued to pursue other employment that would welcome me in the labour market. I succeeded in some although few of them was for a short space of time since I was unhappy with work settings and wages was not so good as well. But nevertheless, I tried to put my head above waters and keep afloat in my desire to pursue my goals to make a living for myself and my son as I was also a single parent.

Jenner is now 36 years old, and he loves to care for dogs as a means of earning a bit of cash. He is very good with these dogs. I sometimes help him out by looking after them when the need arises for when asked to do that and I had found that they are indeed a man's best friend. They are a loving creature that brightens the day. When my mother failed to be there for me through thin and thick, I relied on Jenner's wise counsel to support me and help me overcome my struggles. He is such an adorable young man who loves God with his heart and is also helping others that God brings along his path. I am just lucky to have him around me all the time and I am thrilled to see him grow up over the years.

When things do not seem right, I like to pour out my heart before God and trust in prayer asking him to sort things out for me and help me to get with the task for the day. Therefore, I take a day at a time prayerfully going through all tasks that I need to accomplish as the day wears out. There are sometimes not enough hours in the day to get all these sorts of things done but with the help from above, I am able to do the most I can in all areas of my life and leaving everything to God to work it all out for my good. It is all about getting the balance right with rest and play and determine when I should stop or move forward in each task. I tried to minimize stress a lot because I can easily be stressed out if I am not careful with things. I tried to let God move me on rather than me moving things on my own effort. I need that push from on high and certain that God will bring me out victoriously to overcome all challenges that I may face. As the days go by, I see God's hand of love reaching out to me and helping me to take the initiative to move onto a better life in him and be successful.

I tried to be myself not what society wants me to be or what other people want me to be either. Without him I am lost in the desert place with no one to talk to or to assist me find my way back in life. Thanks be to God for the gift of prayer and worship which is a part of my daily routine. God's anointing is upon me, making straight my rough life and bringing me to a haven of rest in the one I serve that is God almighty. God promises me that he will make a way for me where there seems to be no way and if only, I can see him at work in my life then I will have no other way than to thank him very much for all his loving kindness towards me and my family who care for me.

Poverty attached itself to me but not for too long because I have a God, I serve who provides for my every need. I can now see God's hands at work in my life daily as I pursue my God given talents and use my skills and gifts for his glory. There are times in my life when God remains silent, I am reaching out to him, but he seems too distant from me and I wonder why he left me in suspense and not hearing my cry but silence usually means that God is still working in the process of time to manifest his will. He always makes a way for me whenever I call upon his name, he has been good to me over the years doing me favours at all costs and in al situations.

In those situations of my development, I try to figure out what I can be doing while waiting for God to act upon my behalf. Sometimes I spend time in praise, worship, and thanksgiving because he sees all things and will come through for me if I do not give up and continue worshipping and asking for his name in my situation. It's hard going as I don't know what to expect but since I am serving a God who understands I trust and take him at his word, firmly declaring the promises of God upon my life. That is why I spend time reading the Bible daily and am familiar with the promises of God. The advice I take on board is to always allow God to rule and direct my life because he knows what is best for my life and he will make all things work for my

God if I let him take the driver's seat of my life. It is not always easy to let him rule in my life as the devil seeks me to and fro to devour me, but I have hope in God and what he can do for me makes it all the more easy. I face challenges in my journey of life every now and then but the most important thing to note is that these setbacks have helped to shape my life and give me a new lease of life as I seek to know him more and be obedient to his voice as he speaks to me daily.

I do not allow people or situations to bring me down in life. I know who I am, and I can pursue all the goals and tasks set before me daily. I do not yield to negative talk about my life because God has made me to be real and genuine in my quest to be integrated in this side of the world. He has created me for a purpose and that is to serve him and to be in his kingdom. God is my centre of attraction and I find confidence in his divine care and attention upon my life. Jesus is the author and finisher of my faith, and it gives me so much joy to know that Jesus can sort out my worries if I allow him in my life and crown him Lord and Saviour. I know that better days are ahead of me, and I wait upon God to move in my life as I seek to please him in all that I do in this world. I have no other helper except God on his throne in heaven, he sees and satisfies every longing in my life. I am also very glad because a higher power is at my behest when I need that push in the right direction.

Sometime ago when I was going through a period of depression and didn't know what to do with my life. I suddenly realised the hand of God reaching out to me in love and bringing me out of that state of ill health and restoring my life to full fellowship with him. The journey in my health is so raw with lots of moaning about why and how I came about to suffer from this illness. I put it down to stress and the university workload I was pursuing with at that time somewhere around 1993 which made me to be unable to take my final exam at university. All is not lost, as I am slowly getting things sorted out and wait patiently for the red light to pursue other avenues that is of interest to me. I was actually admitted on two occasions to hospital for this illness because I refused to take medication and was in total denial of the condition but I then finally realised that if I admit the fact that I am ill and take medication prescribed I will be able to recover from it very quickly. This I have done ever since I decide to own up to my sickness.

Chapter 14

Conclusion

I want to take this opportunity to thank God for making it possible to write my story under the guidance of the Holy Spirit because without him in my life this would have been impossible to bring to pass. I am filled with appreciation to the various channels I have come across during my existence in this world, and I am happy to report that things have been going well with me over the few years of existence. All thanks and praise to God who watches every move to make and assist me to get my head around difficult situations.

My whole life has been tough but happy because I included God in every area of my life, although sometimes stubbornness has placed an issue in my life, but I have been able to be brought back to the path of holiness and righteousness ever since I decided to put my trust in the living God.

It has not always been easy, life has been unkind to me sometimes. I am determined now to follow Jesus' teachings no matter what Satan brings my way. He will have to give up the light and go away from my life because I have been sold to Jesus and will continue serving him no matter what tasks I may face.

The light of God is shining within me, and it has also enabled me to be all I can be in this world whilst pursuing my God given skills and also be in the position to pursue a well-balanced life and diet to make me function well in my daily activities. I tend to do lots of walks as that helps me keep fit and gets my whole body balanced properly. I also try to eat a well-balanced diet everyday with 3 course meals. I am also very creative in my desire to invent new ideas and skills to bring to the attention of others.

New ways of reaching out to people in my world and to be always in the position of trust and gratitude.

Every moment that goes by is a time well spent in his presence, so I am very aware of what goes around me from every passing day. I don't let situations put me down or dictate the way life should be for me because I know the God I serve is able to deliver me and use me for his glory. I am always willing to be an instrument in the hands of God so that others too may be drawn unto his presence. The experience I face in life has made me into a new person with lots of shining personality coming through. I am surrounded by loyal people who support me.

There have been very bad relationships I was involved in, leaving me with a broken heart and also to be left on my own to bring up a child as a single parent. But since God is all loving and concerned for me, I had been able to sort out the mess I found myself in and move forward with my life. I am still trusting God to send me my Mr Charming as sometimes I need that other person by my side who shares a similar faith as I do, so I keep praying and trusting that before not too long someone may appear in my life. We are all imperfect people in this life, living in our various houses and doing other things which are interesting but having said that it would be nice of the Lord according to his will to send me a partner who will love me for what I am and not judge or bring me down with their lips. Some of these relationships I have been involved in I've always felt that those men themselves had to deal with issues of life, like insecurity. But if I allow God to make a choice that's fine, I know that his provision is always good and not evil and will bring me hope and satisfaction all the days of my life.

My ex-boyfriend Osborne Marke was in the habit of putting me down with his mouth and I used to feel so sad and unhappy when he was around because he did this sort of thing ever so often. He was good with buying gifts but that's not all in a relationship. I need appreciation and loving care from the person who intends to be my boyfriend and future husband. In fact, we were engaged to be married but after a few of his follies I decided not to pursue the marriage and broke up the relationship. People can be very insensitive to the needs of others and he loved his food and caused me to spend a lot of time in the kitchen, cooking his favourite meals and going to the market to buy the foodstuff. Something I seldom do now; I occasionally visit the market and don't cook everyday but cook once every three days which suits me best.

I am trying to lose weight as I have put on some weight over the lockdown sessions in London recently. I try to eat sensibly and drink lots of water and eat fruit as recommended by my doctor. My doctor is good in that she advises me on issues relating to my health and gives me good, prescribed medication to help with my sickness. She is so kind and understanding someone I can speak to when things are getting out of hand and too much to bear. At least in my opinion there are quite a few people I can talk to when things are getting out of control for me.

I do not take life for granted as I must work hard to get a successful result in whatever I do. Sometimes I shed tears in prayer to achieve it, but it is all worth the effort. Nothing comes by chance as endurance and perseverance are the key notions in all I undertake.

I am a bit disappointed that I applied for a job I thought I would get but was told that after careful consideration my application was unsuccessful. Sad though that is, not getting the job I wanted is not in God's plan for my life and another one more suitable to my needs will become available soon. I am still believing and trusting that God will provide for all my needs. I don't easily give up on my dreams. If I know that God has promised me something I keep pressing on until I get it, so it is all part and parcel of life and the road I should take in my development. Sometimes things just work out easily, other times I tend to meet tackles on the way. But in all these things I believe God is preparing me for something better for his glory so that the praise may go directly to him.

I marvel at his love for me because if it had not been for the good Lord on my side, I don't know what would come at the end of my life, so I am very grateful that he is in my life now more than ever before.

My heart is so filled with worship and thanksgiving to our God for all his wonderful kindness and love showed to me over the years of my existence. He has not let me down. I am glad to be his child and be in his service. I now intercede, professing Christ to others and making him known in all areas of life. A job I don't take lightly because he has saved me for such a time as this and I hope to follow in this trend all the days of my life. God has given me salvation and I lack nothing, I just need to serve honour, obey him, and make him the centre of my life. Things may not go well but keeping up the faith is the key to success because he will surely show up in my situation and give me the victory.

Better days are ahead of me, and I cannot wait to tap into all the blessings that God will bestow upon me as I seek to obey his voice in all areas of my life.

The bottom line for me is know who you trust, and I have come from a humble background to be in the position of trust with my God and allow him to direct every aspect of my life. There have been trials on the way, but I stay focus on God and allow him to oversee my life. I am now reaping the fruits of my labour, having waited all this time for God to move on my behalf. I rent a house in Wimbledon, and I am in a job now, although it can be a little better but all the same, I thank God for small mercies. I am in touch with people who support me and help in whatever needs I have.

I try not to be moved by outside forces, nothing excites me any-more I just follow the lead of the spirit in my heart and obey that still small voice as it ministers to my soul. I am a living witness of what God can do when you trust him. He has proved him-self to me repeatedly and I am glad to be in his kingdom and be-come one of God's children in Wimbledon, London where I live.

The scars of evil I endured at the hands of family members who used and abused me have been healed over time because I found it hard to come to terms with such cruel behaviour and have al-ways been longing for a breakthrough so that God can heal my wounds and restore my whole life back together again in his love. This is so sad, that people I trusted and looked up to and respect-ed could take such advantage of me. But I am thankful that I have now moved on with my life and put my faith and hope in the God I love so dearly, to help and encourage me in every way that seemed possible according to the power which is at work within me through God.

I often tried not to be overwhelmed by fears or doubts as I inter-act with others who are new to my environment and may tend to judge me wrongly and put a label on my life because life is all that one makes out of it. Sometimes the going may be tough but sticking to the right path that God brings my way enables me to see the mighty Lord at work in my situation and then I see vic-tories on the other side of the coin. It's too much sometimes to bear but after careful thought about where I want to be in my life, I concluded that God can as he is, abundantly above to do more greater things that I can ask him or imagine.

Nowadays I serve God fully because he first loved me and showed me his kindness in every area of my life. He demon-strated his love for me by sending his only begotten son to die on the cross for my sins. I am ever so grateful to him for nail-ing my sins on the cross. It was a cruel and evil behaviour, but he went through it all just because he loved me so much. I do appreciate him and want to show gratitude to him by giving my life over to him in true service and fellowship to the calling of God upon my life. God has helped me, and I know that there is more in store for me.

Satan on the other hand has tried to snatch me away from the Lord's hand he has failed in the process. He is still trying but will continue to fail repeatedly because the God I serve is able to deliver me from the hand of the oppressor. Satan never gives up, so I am left with the decision to pursue my God given talent in Christian living and cooperate very well with the Holy Spirit who is my helper to enable me to live a God-fearing life in this world. There are too many things about the future but one thing I know for sure is that I know who holds the future and I know who holds my hands in readiness to do his will in my life and that is God Almighty the creator of the worlds and Jesus Christ my saviour. I have God's spirit living within me directing every path I should take, and I am certain that God in his love and mercy will see me through the various obstacles that I face from time to time. The enemy of my soul is fighting hard to take me away from the path of holiness and Godliness, but I am assured of God's hand upon my life to overcome all struggles and live a more rewarding life in the society to which I belong.

There is a warfare I go through now, but I am aware of God's presence in my life to be stable and confident that God who has begun a good work within me will bring it to a perfect end. Every day is a new day for me, unknown territories I face daily, some good and others bad but one thing I know for sure is that God is on my side and is seeing me through and helping me to overcome things. I take pleasure in praying to God every day because he always answers my prayers and that gives me faith to believe in him more as needs are always provided for and I also see him at work in other people's lives that I have been praying for. I know this sounds strange, but God has never let me down. He always shows up in my life whenever I need him most.

I do not let situations dictate to me the way life should go. I am always attuning to the Holy Spirit to direct me on any given task after prayerfully considering the outcome in advance of it happening. And I take necessary actions in my need to have a positive effect on the task in question. It's always proved worthwhile as sometimes other people just confirmed it to me by their conversations about the issues. I am very grateful that God can speak to me through situations and people alike as I often need a shoulder to cry on if I am feeling overwhelmed and discontented.

The feeling of defeat is far from me because I trust that God will help me and enable me to be more settled in this world and provide all I need to make a better life in his kingdom.

Just as already mentioned, I am very active in my community, doing lots of walks and exercises to keep myself active and eliminate all unnecessary illness from attacking my body. As the cold weather here in London is upon us all I'm beginning to experience pain in my leg again although I am still doing the physio exercises at home and taking medicine. This is part of the wear and tear the doctor says about my health although things with my leg are improving yet I still trust that one day I will have the victory and will finally be made well soon. The physio exercises require me to keep doing the actions for 3-6 months before I can finally be healed. So, I am waiting patiently for such a time to fulfil itself in my life whilst keeping doing the actions every day. I can't wait to be set free from pain. I am praying though those things work out well for me in this area of my life.

I am thankful to my creator for a job, at least it takes me out of the house, and I tend to exercise a lot going to and fro from home to work. Also, I can earn a living and be in the position to pay my bills as I live alone and get no other help from anywhere or anyone to satisfy that need in my life. I am blessed with a job at Raynes Park, working in the evenings. I am very happy in my work as my friends are very supportive and helpful and give me time to sort myself out if there is a need to do this. I am always punctual and reliable although I just started the job in September 2021.

I was living here with Jenner's friends, two people who misused my telephone so when I told them not to use the phone anymore, they insulted me and spoke to me in a disrespectful manner and told me that they were leaving at the end of the month. Now they have moved, and I have been able to keep living costs down because of them both moving out. People are rude and abusive, but I am thankful to God that I did not do anything out of order to them. I told Jenner about their behaviour, and he was shocked at them for treating me in a disrespectful manner after all the kindness I showed to them when they were living here with me. Now I don't want anyone to live with me here anymore except my partner that God will give me in the future, and we ought to get married.

Jenner is very helpful; he was trying to help his friends out to put a roof over their heads, but some people are just too difficult to get along with. Not to worry I am safe now in my home and don't need anyone who will take advantage of my kind nature. I believe I was too nice and kind to them so they thought they could take advantage of me.

The enemy has a way to affect me, especially when I am not aware of his negative actions upon my life. But God who knows everything comes in at the right time to deliver me from harm or anything unpleasant that may occur. I am so glad to know God as my master and friend because if it had not been the Lord on my side I doubt if I would be alive this day, but I am so grateful to him for his unfailing love and care over the years. Every day I live I think of his love and the fact that it is unconditional. It is not what I am but only because he loves me so much he sent his son to die in my place to pay the penalty of sin that I owe.

The experiences I have within close family members are unpredictable in the sense that if they can benefit from me they are very supportive, but if not they prove themselves otherwise.

The family is supposed to be safe and free from competition but in my family people are very envious and jealous of each other and if I have an idea and talk to them about it they tend to respond in a jealous fashion, so now I just do my own thing and leave them out of my life so that later on they will catch up on things themselves and see the positive results coming my way.

I try to cut off all negative people out of my life because life is too good to be around people who do not see things the way God intends them to be for me. So, I only trust just a handful of family because I have been abused before by some male family members and I do lack the trust to continue in that same frame of mind. I don't want to be in touch with people who do not share my beliefs or practices because life can get so serious if one lets things that are negative get in the way.

There are lots of distractions about to keep me off the track of God's plans and his will for my life. One thing I came to realise is that these things are Satan's way to get me to lose my grip upon God, but God is faithful who will not suffer me to bite off more than I can chew. He renders help when I need it most and delivers me from all troubles that may come my way.

I was involved in the occult movement sometime in my life. Consulting mediums and reading my stars in the newspaper to see how my life is going but to no success. I kept wasting my money on these consultations which did not get me nowhere except defeat, loss, and pain.

The new age era is not something I should have been involved with in the first place but Satan knowing his goals got me trapped and glued into this area for almost two years. Life was tough during these times until I decided to turn my life over to God to make a way for me out of this misery and despair. It has not been easy as the mediums were adamant, they never wanted to see me go but I pressed on with the decision and here I am to tell the story of it all. Nothing from their side materialised I was just hooked upon false recommendations. God on the other hand was so loving, speaking to me in that still small voice to turn my life over to him and experience the peace of God and see things change in my life for the better. This I did and now I can say that God is good to me, and his mercy is from everlasting to everlasting to those who seek him with all their hearts. In that time, I lost my focus upon God and put it in mere humans to bring me the help and support I needed. I got involved so badly with consultation that I could hardly get money for my basic needs because whenever I consulted the medium they would welcome me and tell me what I would like to hear and make more and more recommendations for me to follow and act by sending money to them. They were coming so very fast in my life that I decided that this is no life I need to let God have his way and trust him for the unknown future. I therefore lost all that money over a 2-year period of consulting mediums from every area of the world and have lived with the regrets of not allowing God to lead and direct my life in the first place.

Whilst I was with the mediums I was still going to church; I would sit listening to sermon upon sermon but was not taking positive steps to stop consulting them. I was glued to the idea as if a spell was cast upon me. I had to break free from it all through deliverance prayers from the body of Christ and decided that enough was enough. I needed to see my way clear and be in the position to live a peaceful and settled life in the community in which I belong. The devil has a way of getting me hooked up in his schemes and I was a victim of his devices. I thank God now I am delivered from these unhappy things that happened to me and I did make a promise to God that I will never go back to such practices ever again and ask him to help me live the life he has called me to lead in his presence.

An area of concern for me on my journey of life is the issue of becoming a victim of scams. I have been scammed a lot for money over a period of 6 years by people who pretended to give me money that's not theirs in the first place in exchange for me sending them money. At first, I thought this was real but having kept sending more and more money I came to realise that I had just been scammed and made to part with an amount of cash that I would have been able to use wisely in my own area of life or to help other people who God was directing me to assist. These people are thieves and used tactics to deceive me into parting with my money. They would send emails, text or sometimes a phone call to make their request and I thought at that time that they were genuine and sincere. I lost a lot of money and trust in not being able to defend myself.

Another scam I went through is when my bank card was used by people who withdrew monies from my bank account but thankfully the bank gave me back the stolen money and got hold of the people who did this evil. I am very sad at the way people prey on the vulnerable in our society. I was therefore left with no option than to ask God the question 'Why me Lord?' I had been very careful with my bank card and wondered why my card got into the hands of other people.

At one instance the culprit rang me and told me that my card had been used in Aberdeen, which was a lie, and he asked me to give information about my card. I thought then that they were genuine because the man claimed to be from my bank. So, I gave the information; later I discovered that this man has emptied my account. I went to the bank to report it and the matter was under investigation and my money was refunded to my account after a 24-hour period. That's a lot of time to wait for my money to be refunded as I needed to spend it on other things.

Scammers are all over the place and I am careful now when I do transactions so that this sort of thing will not happen to me again. I just wondered where God is in all of this trying to make a living on the one hand and on the other hand someone somewhere is stealing from my resources. I thought I was being careful, but these thieves are so clever they know when to act and they are so successful in robbing me of my hard-earned cash. I was very upset about this sort of behaviour as I believe everyone should be able to make their own living in life and not steal.

Family members who were so close to me and someone I could trust also robbed me of my hard-earned cash. My sister, who is older than me, Daphne, stole an amount of cash from money I sent to her in Sierra Leone through money transfer to give to Jenner's grandmother who is also living in Sierra Leone. She collected the 10,000 and kept it for her own use. This sort of bad behaviour deeply hurt me because as a sibling I did not expect her to act in such a cruel way and she was held a well-paid job in the police force. I think that keeping the peace and living a centred life would be first and foremost in her life. When I asked her about it, she started giving me a silly excuse. I was so sad and ashamed that she could do such a thing to an old lady by depriving her from her gift from me.

Another incident is also when Audrey my younger sister increased the price of Faraway perfume that I usually buy for £8 per bottle to £11. She was assisting a colleague to sell the Avon product and I normally buy it from her for £8. When I declined making the payment of £11 she then turned to me and said, 'Well then pay the amount you usually pay'. I then discovered that she was also taking the opportunity to cash in on Avon sales to me but as God would have it, I wasn't having anything to do with it.

Moreover, my mum travelled to London on vacation in the summer of 1993 for six months from Sierra Leone. Shortly after my dad passed onto glory when she was going back, I went to the shops and bought clothes for my son Jenner who was still living with his dad in Sierra Leone. On her return to Freetown, she never gave the poor child the clothes I sent but instead sold them and kept the money to herself for her own use.

These are family members whom the devil used to bring sadness to my spirit so who do I trust now? When family can be made to do such a thing of mistrust, I don't trust them anymore but instead I have kept a low profile on the issue since that time in question. I have forgiven them for their actions, but I am also protective of myself to guard against any such bad behaviour happening in the future.

There is an evil force behind it all as it seeks to destroy my life and bring misery to my soul.

Only my brother Victor is someone I trust. He has not done anything to me, instead I approach him for money when I am in need, and he has been in the position to help me out.

I know that God will fight my battles for me and give me victory over everyone who used and took advantage of my kind nature. People have been so cruel to me because I come across as a very nice and sincere person. Someone they think has got lots of money when in fact I am only surviving with the little that God gives me daily. I seek his face regularly and trust him to meet my every need and my God in heaven has answered my prayers. The devil puts people who are evil and bad on my pathway but with the armour of God in my hand I will defeat every scheme of evil against my socialisation process in this life.

If family members could treat me in this inhuman way, what can I say if a stranger does the same to me. I am lost for words and feel let down by such behaviour. I take courage in God's word, that is why I am passionate about my hope in God and lean on his promises that when my mother and father abandon me then the Lord will lift me up.

Moreover, people are people, and an evil seed is sown into the hearts of such cruel people who seek to see my downfall. But with confidence and hope I will prevail I don't let situations bring me down in my journey of life. I prevail over Satan the devil and the world. Only Jesus can heal my broken heart, therefore I will continue to trust him for his grace and mercy upon my life. God on the other hand has been good to me. I now live a successful life here in my home in Wimbledon and he has blessed me with finances to enable me to lead a fulfilling life as I seek to serve him and others in my community and across the world. He has also given me a ministry and that is to pray as an intercessor for the people of the earth. A task I don't take lightly but pursue every challenge and test that goes into being a victorious servant of the highest God.

God has not left me as an orphan but has been meeting my needs according to his riches in glory and I am glad that I belong to the family of God now and can only say that my walk with God has been pleasant and rewarding, overcoming every trial that I face and see the hand of God at work in my life as I am able to acquire wealth in all its fulness to the praise and adoration of God.

I am determined and have made up my mind that nothing shall let me forsake the availing of my God upon my life because all that matters now for me is to live life to the full and serve my people across the globe.

My sister Audrey keeps saying false things about me, but I don't allow that to distract me from the knowledge I have about my God. He can shut the mouth of the lions on my behalf. She does not know who she is dealing with. A servant and saint of the highest God redeemed, blessed and created for such a time as this. I am also very grateful to God for making me see the other side of life and will continue to seek his face daily and become all I can be. My God will fight my battles and give unto me the victory repeatedly. I try to live a quiet life at Sycamore Road and continue to serve God and make his presence felt in my life and I worship him in spirit and in truth. Nothing comes by chance, and I don't want to take no for an answer when God promises me health, wealth, and friendship in all its fullness.

I know that all families have issues that they have to contend with, but my own family is worse. I suffered grossly at the hands of people I trusted and looked up to in life. Only God sees my heart, I was sincere in my dealings with them, but they took advantage of me and made a fortune out of my life. Furthermore, because the force of evil and Satan on the one hand is having his way in my situation by blaming me for all that happened but as God would have it, I survived the ordeal and hope for a better life doing the service of the Lord and serve him to the best of my ability.

I will never forget when I went to a prayer meeting, came home and the house had been broken into. I was devastated and upset at such a cruel thing happening to me, but God remained faithful even though they stole my belongings yet still God provided for my needs and brought people along my path who gave me some of the things that I needed at that time. God is good when you pray, and bad things happen. God knows it all and today I can say that God is my Jehovah Jireh, he provides and makes a way for me where there seems to be no way. I am happy as Larry now and I am confident that my God will continue to uphold and bless me beyond all measure.

God is still blessing me no matter what Satan thinks of me. I will continue to serve the Almighty God for all his wonderful works towards me and the people who care about me. I am certain that one day I will be in the position to be set free from all these sad happenings and be in touch with my true self to be able to pass on my story to others so that they too may see what has transpired in my life over the past 61 years of existence on planet Earth.

The author

Juliet Smith was born in London but spent most
of her early life in Sierra Leone. Later she returned
to London and settled down to a life of hard
work, but became a victim of racism, crime and
bigotry. She was abused, both in London and
Sierra Leone. However, her faith in God has kept
her going, and though she has sometimes strayed
from the way of the Lord, she has always found
her way back into the fold.

Juliet lives in Wimbledon and is an enthusiastic
churchgoer, as well as an avid listener to
Christian radio. She has a qualification in Business
Administration from Sierra Leone but has found
it difficult to establish a career in the UK. Even so,
Juliet finds meaning in the work she can find.
Despite having suffered great hardship, Juliet's
faith in God has led her to see the positive side
of life. She takes great delight in her grown-up
son Jenner as well as her fellow churchgoers, to
whom she is eternally grateful. She serves her
community in Wimbledon as an active volunteer
for a variety of church projects.

The publisher

*He who stops
getting better
stops being good.*

This is the motto of novum publishing, and our focus
is on finding new manuscripts, publishing them and
offering long-term support to the authors.
Our publishing house was founded in 1997, and since
then it has become THE expert for new authors and
has won numerous awards.

**Our editorial team will peruse each manuscript
within a few weeks free of charge and without
obligation.**

You will find more information about
novum publishing and our books on the internet:

w w w . n o v u m - p u b l i s h i n g . c o . u k